Making Your Case

Making Your Case
The Art of Persuading Judges

Antonin Scalia & Bryan A. Garner

Published by Thomson/West
610 Opperman Drive
P.O. Box 64526
St. Paul, MN 55164-0527
1-800-328-9352

IBSN 978-0-314-18471-9

Printed in the United States of America

Library-of-Congress Cataloguing-in-Publication Data
Antonin Scalia & Bryan A. Garner
Making your case: the art of persuading judges — 1st ed.
          p.   cm.
Includes bibliographical references and index.
1. Law — United States — Methodology.
2. Appellate procedure — United States.
3. Oral pleading — United States.
4. Legal composition.
5. Forensic rhetoric.
I. Scalia, Antonin, 1936–.
I. Garner, Bryan A., 1958–.
II. Title

Page design by Jeff Newman
    Body Copy: Adobe Jenson 13/15
    Section Headings: Myriad Pro Semibold 12/14
    Inset Quotations: Myriad Pro Condensed 10/10.5

Third printing

"Experience is undoubtedly a great teacher, yet it may be counterproductive if what has been cultivated and refined are bad habits. The point is that excellence is the product of the diligent study and application of sound principles, not simply the accumulation of time logged in . . . courts."

—T.W. Wakeling (1979)

Even so:

"No rules in the handbooks are capable in themselves of making brilliant performances out of those who intend to dispense with practice and exercise."

—Dionysius of Halicarnassus (ca. 30 B.C.)

To our parents

S. Eugene Scalia
(1903–1986)

Catherine L. Scalia
(1905–1985)

Gary Thomas Garner
(b. 1930)

Mariellen Griffin Garner
(1931–1994)

Acknowledgments

During various stages of the development of our manuscript, we've benefited from the generosity of many readers with great experience in our subject:

Hon. Susan Agid
Richard D. Bernstein, Esq.
Hon. Paul G. Cassell
Karolyne H. Cheng, Esq.
Jordan B. Cherrick, Esq.
Charles Dewey Cole Jr., Esq.
Richard M. Coleman, Esq.
Prof. Edward H. Cooper
Prof. Ross Davies
Prof. Michael R. Devitt
Brian J. Donato, Esq.
Prof. William V. Dorsaneo III
David M. Dorsen, Esq.
Hon. Frank H. Easterbrook
Hon. Martin L.C. Feldman
Stephen F. Fink, Esq.
Hon. Arthur J. Gajarsa
Henry Goldberg, Esq.
Carl F. Goodman, Esq.
Michael A. Hatchell, Esq.
Prof. Geoffrey C. Hazard Jr.
Hon. Nathan L. Hecht
Hon. Robert H. Henry
Steven A. Hirsch, Esq.

Tiger Jackson, Esq.
Hon. Edith Hollan Jones
Prof. Susan Karamanian
George M. Kryder, Esq.
Prof. Douglas Laycock
Todd E. Macaluso, Esq.
Paul G. McNamara, Esq.
Brian Melendez, Esq.
Jeff Newman, Esq.
Gloria C. Phares, Esq.
Hon. Thomas M. Reavley
Eugene Scalia, Esq.
Ann Taylor Schwing, Esq.
Hon. Laurence H. Silberman
Joseph F. Spaniol Jr., Esq.
Scott P. Stolley, Esq.
Hon. Jeffrey S. Sutton
Hon. Deanell R. Tacha
Randall M. Tietjen, Esq.
Prof. John R. Trimble
Aaron Van Oort, Esq.
Richard S. Walinski, Esq.
Prof. Sir David Williams
Hon. Diane P. Wood

For their perceptive comments and suggestions, we're most grateful.

Copious thanks are also due to Professor Roy M. Mersky of the University of Texas School of Law. He and his incomparable staff at the Tarlton Law Library, especially Jeanne Price and Leslie Ashbrook, proved critically helpful in tracking down background sources for us to consult in our research.

Karen Magnuson of Portland, Oregon, proofread the book in her typically fastidious way—for which we're appreciative.

A.S.
B.A.G.

Contents

Contents

Contents

Contents

Foreword

Published advice on how to persuade judges is as old as the profession of judging itself. Its sources include Aristotle, Isocrates, Demetrius, Cicero, and Quintilian. So anything fundamentally new contributed by this small volume would probably be wrong. Our purpose is to make the best earlier advice—with perhaps a few suggestions of our own—readily available to the modern practitioner and to adapt it to the circumstances of modern American litigation.

Unsurprisingly, respected authorities on the art of judicial persuasion are not always unanimous. Where there is substantial disagreement with our recommendations, we acknowledge it. Indeed, on four salient points, we've acknowledged disagreements between the two of us, leaving readers to make up their own minds, as they inevitably will.

We deal here with both written and oral presentation. Since many points that apply to the one apply equally to the other, we have sought to minimize repetition by presenting preliminary sections dealing with the basics of argumentation—knowing your audience, syllogistic reasoning, etc.—and then offering separate sections first on brief-writing, stressing the peculiarities of that form, and then on oral argument doing the same.

To lighten the journey, we have adopted a conversational style that includes occasional contractions and remarks more flippant or colloquial than one would normally encounter in legal commentary. The reader who feels that some of these indulgences fall short of the formality and sobriety expected of a jurist should attribute all of them to the other author, and assume that they have been included under protest.

A.S.
B.A.G.

Introduction

Judges can be persuaded only when three conditions are met:

(1) They must have a clear idea of what you're asking the court to do.

(2) They must be assured that it's within the court's power to do it.

(3) After hearing the reasons for doing what you are asking, and the reasons for doing other things or doing nothing at all, they must conclude that what you're asking is best—both in your case and in cases that will follow.

To provide the reasons that will persuade the court to conclude in your favor, you must know what *motivates* the court, and that's not always easy to discern. To be sure, following precedent is a concern for all judges, especially in the lower courts. So you must always seek to persuade the court that the disposition you urge is required by prior cases—or at the very least is not excluded by them.

Beyond stare decisis, however, it becomes a matter of some speculation what motivates a particular judge. In a question of first impression, to be resolved within a court's common-law powers, *all* judges would agree that the decision must be driven by (1) fairness to the litigants and a socially desirable result in the case at hand, and (2) adoption of a legal rule that will provide fairness, socially desirable results, and predictability in future cases. How much weight a particular judge may give to (1) or (2)—or to their subparts—may vary. But all judges will surely give *some* weight to all those considerations, and you can be confident that you're not wasting your time in addressing them.

But unconstrained common-law decision-making is an increasing rarity. Courts are usually confronted with interpreting a governing text, whether a constitutional provision, a statute, an agency regulation, or a municipal ordinance. And in these cases, what motivates a judge cannot be so readily determined. Some judges believe that their duty is quite simply to give the text its most natural meaning—in the context of related provisions, of course, and applying the usual canons of textual interpretation—without assessing the desirability of the consequences that meaning produces. At the other extreme are those judges who believe it their duty to give the text whatever permissible meaning will produce the most desirable results. Most judges probably fall somewhere between these two extremes, perhaps adopting the most natural meaning except when policy consequences affect an area that they consider particularly important (e.g., environmental protection or sex discrimination), or perhaps consulting policy consequences only when the most natural meaning is not entirely clear. Unless you know for sure what sort of judge you're dealing with, you're well advised to argue (if possible) *both* most-natural-meaning *and* policy-consequences-*cum*-permissible-meaning.

Introduction

As we'll discuss in some detail, your arguments must make logical sense. Your legal and factual premises must be well founded, and your reasoning must logically compel your conclusion. But while computers function solely on logic, human beings do not. All sorts of extraneous factors—emotions, biases, preferences—can intervene, most of which you can do absolutely nothing about (except play upon them, if you happen to know what they are).

An ever-present factor, however, and one that you can always influence, is the human proclivity to be more receptive to argument from a person who is both trusted and liked. All of us are more apt to be persuaded by someone we admire than by someone we detest. In the words of Isocrates: "[T]he man who wishes to persuade people will not be negligent as to the matter of character; he will apply himself above all to establish a most honourable name among his fellow-citizens; for who does not know that words carry greater conviction when spoken by a man of good repute?"[1] Aristotle further noted that character makes a special difference on disputed points: "We believe good men more fully and more readily than others: this is true . . . where exact certainty is impossible and opinions are divided."[2]

Your objective in every argument, therefore, is to show yourself worthy of trust and affection. Trust is lost by dissembling or conveying false information—not just inten-

---

1   Isocrates, *Antidosis* (ca. 353 B.C.; George Norlin trans.), in *Readings in Classical Rhetoric* 47, 49 (Thomas W. Benson & Michael H. Prosser eds., 1988).

2   Aristotle, *Rhetoric*, Book 1, ch. 2 (ca. 330 B.C.), in *Rhetoric and Poetics of Aristotle* 25 (W. Rhys Roberts & Ingram Bywater trans., 1954).

tionally but even carelessly; by mischaracterizing precedent to suit your case; by making arguments that could appeal only to the stupid or uninformed; by ignoring rather than confronting whatever weighs against your case. Trust is won by fairly presenting the facts of the case and honestly characterizing the issues; by owning up to those points that cut against you and addressing them forthrightly; and by showing respect for the intelligence of your audience.

As for affection, you show yourself to be likable by some of the actions that inspire trust, and also by the lack of harsh combativeness in your briefing and oral argument, the collegial attitude you display toward opposing counsel, your refusal to take cheap shots or charge misbehavior, your forthright but unassuming manner and bearing at oral argument—and, perhaps above all, your even-tempered good humor. Some people, it must be said, are inherently likable. If you're not, work on it. (It may even improve your social life.)

General Principles
of Argumentation

1. Be sure that the tribunal has jurisdiction.

Nothing is accomplished by trying to persuade someone who lacks the authority to do what you're asking — whether it's a hotel clerk with no discretion to adjust your bill or a receptionist who cannot bind the company to the contract you propose. Persuasion directed to an inappropriate audience is ineffective.

So it is with judges, whose authority to act has many limitations—jurisdictional limits—relating to geography, citizenship of the parties, monetary amount, and subject matter. From justices of the peace to justices of supreme courts, judges face as a first task to be sure of their authority to decide the matters brought before them and to issue the orders requested. If they don't have that authority in your case, you don't just have a weak case, you have no case at all.

Most weak points in your case will be noted by opposing counsel, giving you a chance to reflect on them and respond. If opposing counsel does not protest a particular point, the defect will often be regarded as waived. But a defect in subject-matter jurisdiction is a different matter altogether. An opposing party often has no interest in challenging jurisdiction, being as eager as you are to have the court resolve the dispute. But in many courts (including all federal courts), absence of subject-matter jurisdiction, unlike most other defects, cannot be waived. And in some of those courts (including all federal courts), even if no party raises the issue, the court itself can and must notice it. Nothing is more disconcerting, or more destructive of your argument, than to hear these words from the bench: "Counsel, before we proceed any further, tell us why this court has jurisdiction over this case." You need a convincing answer to this question—and preferably a quick and short one—or else you're likely, in the picturesque words of the lawyer's cliché, to be poured out of court.

Two caveats about jurisdiction: (1) Jurisdictional rules apply in appellate courts as well as in trial courts. The Supreme Court of the United States, for example, has jurisdiction over a state-court decision (involving a federal question) only when that decision is final, and only when there is no adequate and independent state-law ground for the judgment. (2) Defendants and appellees are much more likely to ignore jurisdictional requirements than are plaintiffs and appellants. But jurisdiction is just as important to them, and they must attend to it.

The rules of the Supreme Court of the United States require briefs to set forth, immediately after the description of the parties, the basis for the Court's jurisdiction. Even if the court before which you are appearing has no similar rule, it's good practice to pretend that it does and to identify the law, and the facts, that render this original action, or this appeal, properly brought before that court. Keep that information handy in case the court asks.

2. Know your audience.

A good lawyer tries to learn as much as possible about the judge who will decide the case. The most important information, of course, concerns the judge's judicial philosophy—what it is that leads this particular judge to draw conclusions. Primarily text, or primarily policy? Is the judge strict or lax on stare decisis? Does the judge love or abhor references to legislative history? The best place to get answers to such questions is from the horse's mouth: read the judge's opinions, particularly those dealing with matters relevant to your case. Also read the judge's articles and speeches on relevant subjects.

Besides judicial philosophy, learn all you can about how the judge runs the courtroom. Is the judge unusually impatient? If so, you might want to pare down your arguments to make them especially terse and pointed. Is the judge an old-school stickler for decorum? If so, you might refer to opposing counsel as "my friend." One federal judge had a practice of fining counsel $20 (no notice in advance) for placing a briefcase on the counsel table. It's good to know of such peculiarities. Some of these courtroom characteristics you can (and should)

> "It may surprise you, but many firms keep 'book' on all the judges before whom they appear. This book includes much more than a biographical sketch which you might find in *Who's Who*: Does the judge listen with patience, or does he seem absorbed in other matters or half asleep? Does he treat the government as just another litigant, or does the government have a preferred or, sometimes, a prejudiced position? Does he seem impressed by the reputation or prestige of the lawyer making the argument? These and many other impressions are recorded for future reference."
> —Samuel E. Gates

observe by sitting in on one of the judge's hearings. Beyond that, however, talk to colleagues at the bar who are familiar with the judge's idiosyncrasies.

Finally, learn as much as you readily can about the judge's background. Say you're appearing before Judge Florence Kubitzky. With a little computer research and asking around, you discover that fly-fishing is her passion; that her father died when she was only seven; that her paternal grandparents, who were both professors at a local college, took charge of her upbringing; that she once chaired the state Democratic Party; that she enjoys bridge; that she has been estranged from her brother and sister for many years; that she graduated from Mount Holyoke College and took her law degree from the University of Michigan; that she's an aficionado of good wines; that her favorite restaurant is the Beaujolais Room; that she was counsel for a craft union before coming to the bench; and so on. Going in, all these data seem irrelevant to how the judge might decide your breach-of-contract case, but you might well find some unpredictable uses for this knowledge over the course of a lengthy trial. You might want to stress, for example, that the defective contract performance your client is complaining about violated basic standards of the craft and reflects shoddy workmanship. At the very least, these details will humanize the judge for you, so that you will be arguing to a human being instead of a chair.

Apart from judges' personal characteristics, there are also characteristics of individual courts. Can the appellate court you are appearing before be relied on to read the briefs before hearing argument? If not, you might devote more argument time to the facts than you otherwise would, or deal with some legal points that are so basic that you'd normally pass over them in oral argument. Is it the practice of the appellate court to assign the opinion to a particular judge before the case is even argued? If so, you can probably assume less familiarity with the facts and issues on the part of the other judges, and you might want to lay out your argument in a more rudimentary fashion for their benefit. Is the court notoriously dismissive of higher-court precedent? Stress the public-policy benefits of your proposed disposition.

Bear in mind that trial judges are fundamentally different from appellate judges. They focus on achieving the proper result in one particular case, not on crafting a rule of law that will do justice in the generality of cases. And they will pursue that objective principally through their treatment of the facts (if the case is tried to the court) and discretionary rulings. In most jurisdictions, trial judges are more disposed than appellate judges to strict observance of governing caselaw—perhaps because their work is subject to mandatory review. So at the trial-court level you are well advised to spend more time on the facts and on the discussion of precedent (from the relevant courts) and less time on policy arguments. That's one reason why a good trial brief can rarely be used before an appellate court without major changes.

3. Know your case.

Have you ever tried buying equipment from a salesperson who didn't know beans about it? You might understandably have fled the store. Although lawyers aren't selling equipment, they are selling their cases.

Judges listen to counsel because, at the time of briefing or argument, counsel can be expected to know more about the legal and factual aspects of the case than anyone else. But if it becomes clear that this is not so, judicial attention will flag. If you're asked about a fact in the record that you're ignorant of, or a clearly relevant case that you're unfamiliar with and have failed to mention in your brief, don't expect the court to give your argument much weight. Your very first assignment, therefore, is to become an expert on the facts and the law of your case. If you're a senior partner who hasn't the time to do this, assign the case to the junior partner or associate who knows it best.

> "I am constantly amazed, during Supreme Court arguments, to hear an attorney virtually struck dumb by questions from the bench that anyone with any knowledge of the case should have anticipated. It is as if the attorney has become so imbued with the spirit of his cause that he has totally blinded himself to the legitimate concerns that someone else might have in adopting his position."
> —E. Barrett Prettyman Jr.

At the appellate stage, knowing your case means, first and foremost, knowing the record. You never know until it is too late what damage a gap in your knowledge of the record can do—not only at oral argument (see § 62), but even in your brief. Richard Bernstein of Washington, D.C., tells of a case in which the plaintiff-appellees, represented by a prominent firm first retained on the appeal, made the theoretically plausible argument that one reason they should receive an injunction for patent infringement was that damages were difficult to prove. Unfortunately, as the appellant's reply brief carefully (oh-so-carefully) explained, the appellee's own expert had told the jury that in this case damages were easy to prove and calculate. Needless to say, the appellee did not press the point at oral argument.

Don't underestimate the importance of facts. To be sure, you will be arguing to the court about the law, but what law applies—what cases are in point, and what cases can be distinguished—depends ultimately on the facts of your case. If you're arguing an appeal, you must have a firm grasp of what facts have been determined below or must be accepted as true, and what facts are still unresolved.

Knowing a case also means knowing exactly what you're asking for—and how far short of that mark you can go without bringing back to your client a hollow victory. Say a member of an appellate panel asks, "Counsel, if we agree with your petition, would you be content with a remand for the lower court to consider X, an issue not decided below and not briefed or argued here?" You must know whether your opponent ever raised that issue below. If not, you must insist on outright reversal and entry of judgment in your favor. If you fail to do so, the court may cite your failure as a concession that your adversary hasn't forfeited the issue. If, however, your adversary raised the point but the lower court didn't reach it, you should graciously concede that remand is a possibility but go on to explain why the appellate court should reject that disposition—as by showing, for example, that the facts could not possibly support a judgment on that ground. By conceding what must be conceded, you establish your credentials as a reliable and even-handed counselor.

4. Know your adversary's case.

No general engages the enemy without a battle plan based in large part on what the enemy is expected to do. Your case must take into account the points the other side is likely to make. You must have a clear notion of which ones can be swallowed (accepted but shown to be irrelevant) and which must be vigorously countered on the merits. If your brief and argument come first, you must decide which of your adversary's points are so significant that they must be addressed in your opening presentation and which ones can be left to your reply brief or oral rebuttal. Of course, a principal brief or argument that is all rebuttal is anathema.

At the trial stage, you must initially discern your adversary's positions from the pleadings, the conferences, and discovery, and by using common sense. At the appellate stage, you can rely on what was argued and sought to be proved below. Bear in mind, however, that lawyers tend to develop new arguments, and revise their theories, as the case proceeds upward. Constantly ask yourself what *you* would argue if you were on the other side.

Don't delude yourself. Try to discern the real argument that an intelligent opponent would make, and don't replace it with a straw man that you can easily dispatch.

5. Pay careful attention to the applicable standard of decision.

The separate issues involved in your case may be subject to varying presumptions and burdens of proof. In a criminal trial, the prosecution must establish guilt beyond a reasonable doubt. An adversary who seeks to overturn the judgment you obtained below on the basis of an erroneous jury instruction to which there was no objection must establish not just error but plain error. An appellant who attempts to set aside federal-agency action as contrary to statutory authority must often show not merely that the best reading of the statute favors reversal, but that the agency's reading is not even within the bounds of reason. And so forth.

When the standard of decision favors your side of the case, emphasize that point at the outset of your discussion of the issue—and keep it before the court throughout. Don't let the discussion slide into the assumption that you and your adversary are on a level playing field when in fact the standard of review favors you. Say, for example, that you are asked, in a case involving review of federal-agency action favoring your client, whether you don't think an interpretation of the statute different from the agency's makes more sense. You should respond somewhat as follows: "I don't think so, Your Honor, but it really makes no difference.

The question here is whether the agency's interpretation is a reasonable one, not whether it is the very best. And on that point there is little room for doubt." Remind the court of the favorable standard of review in your summation.

Appellees' briefs commonly treat the standard of review in boilerplate fashion. If your opponent is fighting against a clearly-erroneous or arbitrary-and-capricious standard, make a big deal of it. Point out that the appellant is attempting to retry the case, or to have the court of appeals substitute its judgment for that of the district court or the agency. Say this explicitly, not only in your standard-of-review section but in your introduction and summary of argument.

When the standard of decision is against you, acknowledge the difficulty but demonstrate concretely why the standard is met. Go beyond mere repetition of stock phrases. For example, if you're arguing that the judgment below was clearly erroneous, it does little good to say, "Here one does indeed have a definite and firm conviction that a mistake has been made." Cite a case in which an appellant met that standard and compare it to your own.

The standard of decision is particularly important when you're selecting the issues to pursue on appeal. Appealing a minor error that will be reviewed under an abuse-of-discretion standard will probably do nothing but divert time and attention from your stronger points. Sometimes, too, you can escape or neutralize the more lenient standard of review by framing your claim differently—as by arguing not that the lower court abused its discretion, but that it made an error of law in considering certain factors.

6. Never overstate your case. Be scrupulously accurate.

Once you have worked long and hard on your case—and have decided not to settle—you'll probably be utterly convinced that your side is right. That is as it should be. But the judges haven't worked on the case as long (or, probably, as hard) and are likely, initially at least, to think it much more of a horse race than you do. That will be true in any case, but especially when discretionary review has been granted to resolve a divergence of views in the lower courts. You'll harm your credibility—you'll be written off as a blowhard—if you characterize the case as a lead-pipe cinch with nothing to be said for the other side. Even if you think that to be true, and even if you're right, keep it to yourself. Proceed methodically to show the merits of your case and the defects of your opponent's—and let the abject weakness of the latter speak for itself.

Scrupulous accuracy consists not merely in never making a statement you know to be incorrect (that is mere honesty), but also in never making a statement

> "Nothing, perhaps, so detracts from the force and persuasiveness of an argument as for the lawyer to claim more than he is reasonably entitled to claim. Do not 'stretch' cases cited and relied upon too far, making them appear to cover something to your benefit they do not cover. Do not try to dodge or minimize unduly the facts which are against you. If one cannot win without doing this—and it is seldom he can by doing it—the case should not be appealed."
> —Hon. Wiley B. Rutledge

you are not *certain* is correct. So err, if you must, on the side of understatement, and flee hyperbole. Since absolute negatives are hard to prove, and hence hard to be sure of, you should rarely permit yourself an unqualified "never." Preface a clause like "Such a suit has never been brought in this jurisdiction" with an introductory phrase like "As far as we have been able to discover, ..."

Inaccuracies can result from either deliberate misstatement or carelessness. Either way, the advocate suffers a grave loss of credibility from which it's difficult to recover.

7.   If possible, lead with your strongest argument.

When logic permits, put your winning argument up front in your affirmative case. Why? Because first impressions are indelible. Because when the first taste is bad, one is not eager to drink further. Because judicial attention will be highest at the outset. Because in oral argument, judges' questioning may prevent you from ever getting beyond your first point.

Sometimes, of course, the imperatives of logical exposition demand that you first discuss a point that is not your strongest. For example, serious jurisdictional questions must be discussed first: it makes no sense to open with the merits, and then to consider, at the end, whether the court has any business considering the merits. There is also a logical order of addressing merits issues. C may not be relevant unless B is established, which in turn is not relevant until A has been established. For example, you might have to prove that (A) the agency validly promulgated the regulation, (B) the agency has interpreted the regulation to favor your client, and (C) the agency's interpretation is entitled to judicial deference. No other order of progression would make sense. Similarly, in defending a medical-malpractice judgment on appeal, your argument portion would not begin by justifying the amount of the award and then proceed to defending the judgment of liability.

If you're the appellant, even though logic has pushed your strongest argument toward the back of the line in your principal brief, bring it up front in your reply—which will often set the agenda for the oral argument.

And if you're an appellant at oral argument, begin with your strongest point regardless of what logical progression demands (see § 81). If the court wants logical progression at oral argument, it won't be shy about asking you to turn to a logically prior point; and there (unlike in briefing or bridge), if you don't show your ace of trumps first, you may never get a chance to play it.

8. If you're the first to argue, make your positive case and then preemptively refute in the middle—not at the beginning or end.

It's an age-old rule of advocacy that the first to argue must refute in the middle, not at the beginning or the end. Refuting first puts you in a defensive posture; refuting last leaves the audience focused on your opponent's arguments rather than your own.

So for the first to argue, refutation belongs in the middle. Aristotle observed that "in court one must begin by giving one's own proofs, and then meet those of the opposition by dissolving them and tearing them up before they are made."[3]

Anticipatory refutation is essential for five reasons. First, any judge who thinks of these objections even before your opponent raises them will believe that you've overlooked the obvious problems with your argument. Second, at least with respect to the obvious objections, responding only after your opponent raises them makes it seem as though you are reluctant, rather than eager, to confront them.

> "Every argument is refuted in one of these ways: either one or more of its assumptions are not granted; or if the assumptions are granted, it is denied that a conclusion follows from them; or the form of argument is shown to be fallacious; or a strong argument is met by one equally strong or stronger."
> —Cicero

Third, by systematically demolishing counterarguments, you turn the tables and put your opponent on the defensive. Fourth, you seize the chance to introduce the opposing argument in your own terms and thus to establish the context for later discussion. Finally, you seem more evenhanded and trustworthy.

But anticipatory refutation has its perils. You don't want to refute (and thereby disclose) an argument that your opponent wouldn't otherwise think of. Avoiding this pitfall requires good lawyerly judgment.

---

3 *Rhetoric* ch. 3.17, at 257 (ca. 350 B.C.; H.C. Lawson-Tancred trans., 1991; repr. 2004).

9. If you're arguing after your opponent, design the order of positive case and refutation to be most effective according to the nature of your opponent's argument.

Aristotle advised responding advocates to rebut forcefully in their opening words:

> [I]f one speaks second, one must first address the opposite argument, refuting it and anti-syllogizing, and especially if it has gone down well; for just as the mind does not accept a subject of prejudice in advance, in the same way neither does it accept a speech if the opponent seems to have spoken well. One must therefore make space in the listener for the speech to come; and this will be done by demolishing the opponent's case; thus, having put up a fight against either all or the greatest or most specious or easily refuted points of the opponent, one should move on to one's own persuasive points.[4]

This point applies to those who oppose motions, to respondents, and to appellees. If an opponent has said something that seems compelling, you must quickly demolish that position to make space for your own argument.

Caution: As a general matter, this advice applies to refutation of separate points that make your affirmative points academic—not to your opponent's contesting of your affirmative points themselves. If, for example, your case rests on the proposition that a particular statute creates a claim, you would not begin by refuting your opponent's argument that no claim was created; you would present your own

---

4 *Id.*

affirmative case to the contrary first. Suppose, however, that your opponent has argued, quite persuasively, that the court lacks jurisdiction and that the statute of limitations on any claim has expired. Judges don't like to do any more work than necessary. If they have a fair notion that they will never have to reach the question whether a claim was created, they aren't going to pay close attention to your oral argument on that point. And we have known judges to skip entirely over the merits section of the appellee's brief to reach the response to the appellant's jurisdictional or other nonmerits argument. You must clear the underbrush—or, as Aristotle puts it, "make space"—so that the court will be receptive to your principal argument.

Having made that space, however, you must then fill it. Proceed quickly to a discussion of *your* take on the case, *your* major premise, and *your* version of the central facts. As put by a perceptive observer, in the context of an appellee's argument:

> Nothing could be a more serious mistake than merely to answer the arguments made by counsel for the appellant. These arguments may be skillfully designed to lead counsel for the respondent off into the woods or they may lead him there unintentionally. The proper line of attack for counsel for the respondent to adopt is to proceed to demonstrate by his discussion of the law and the facts that the judgment is right and that it should be affirmed. All other considerations are secondary.[5]

---

5 Harold R. Medina, *The Oral Argument on Appeal*, 20 ABA J. 139, 142–43 (1934).

10. Occupy the most defensible terrain.

Select the most easily defensible position that favors your client. Don't assume more of a burden than you must. If, for example, a leading case comes out differently from your desired result, don't argue that it should be overruled if there is a reasonable basis for distinguishing it. If you're arguing for a new rule in a case of first impression, frame a narrow rule that is consistent with judgment for your client. (Why set yourself the task of providing a satisfactory answer to 100 hypothetical questions about the multifarious effects of a broad rule when you can limit the questions to 5 about the limited effects of a narrow one?) If the defendant has intentionally injured your client in some novel fashion, argue for the existence of some hitherto unrecognized intentional tort, not for a rule that includes negligent acts as well.

Taking the high ground does not mean being noncommittal— saying, for example, that you win under any of three different possible rules, without taking a position about which rule is best. The judge writing an opinion,

> "If your court is divided philosophically, . . . your best bet is to strive for a narrow fact-bound ruling that will not force one or two judges to revisit old battles or reopen old wounds. . . . You want to win unanimously; you do not want a messy dissent to provoke a petition for en banc or even certiorari. On a divided court, big forward or backward (depending on your point of view) leaps in the law come usually only in en bancs, or if they do come in a panel, often end up in en bancs. Take your narrow, 'for this case only' holding, hug it to your bosom, and run."
> —Hon. Patricia M. Wald

especially an appellate judge, cannot indulge that luxury, but must say what the law is. Be helpful. Sure, point out that you win under various rules, but specify what the rule ought to be. If you fail to do that, you leave the impression that all your proposed rules are problematic.

Don't let your adversary's vehement attacks on your moderate position drive you to less defensible ground. If, for example, your position is that an earlier case is distinguishable, don't get muscled into suggesting that it be overruled. And don't let your adversary get away with recharacterizing your position to make it more extreme (a common ploy). If you are arguing, for example, that lawful resident aliens are entitled to certain government benefits, don't leave unanswered your opponent's suggestion that you would reward illegal aliens. Respond at the first opportunity.

On rare occasions it may be in the institutional interest of your client to argue for a broader rule than is necessary to win the case at hand. When you take this tack, the court is likely to ask why it should go so far when a much narrower holding will dispose of the case. Have an answer.

11. Yield indefensible terrain—ostentatiously.

Don't try to defend the indefensible. If a legal rule favoring your outcome is exceedingly difficult to square with the facts of your case, forget about it. You will have to consume an inordinate amount of argument time defending it against judges' attacks, and you will convey an appearance of unreasonableness (not to say desperation) that will damage your whole case.

Rarely will all the points, both of fact and of law, be in your favor. Openly acknowledge the ones that are against you. In fact, if you're the appellant, run forth to meet the obvious ones. In your opening brief, raise them candidly and explain why they aren't dispositive. Don't leave it to the appellee to bring them to the court's attention. Fessing up at the outset carries two advantages. First, it avoids the impression that you have tried to sweep these unfavorable factors under the rug. Second, it demonstrates that, reasonable person that you are, you have carefully considered these matters but don't regard them as significant.

> "[G]rasp your nettles firmly. No matter how unfavorable the facts are, they will hurt you more if the court first learns them from your opponent. To gloss over a nasty portion of the record is not only somewhat less than fair to the court, it is definitely harmful to the case. Draw the sting of unpleasant facts by presenting them yourself."
> —Frederick Bernays Wiener

Suppose, however, that you're the appellee and those damaging points have already been noted by your adversary. Don't pass them by in sullen silence. Make a virtue of a necessity. Boldly proclaim your acceptance of them—thereby demonstrating your fairness, your generosity, and your confidence in the strength of your case, and burnishing your image as an eminently reasonable advocate: "We concede, Your Honor, that no notice was given in this case. The facts cannot be read otherwise." (*Huzzah!* thinks the court. *An even-handed fellow!*) You then go on, of course, to explain why the conceded point makes no difference or why other factors outweigh it.

Bear in mind that a weak argument does more than merely dilute your brief. It speaks poorly of your judgment and thus reduces confidence in your other points. As the saying goes, it is like the 13th stroke of a clock: not only wrong in itself, but casting doubt on all that preceded it.

12. Take pains to select your best arguments. Concentrate your fire.

The most important—the very most important—step you will take in any presentation, whether before a trial court or an appellate court, is selecting the arguments that you'll advance. A mediocre advocate defending a good position will beat an excellent advocate defending a bad position nine times out of ten. (We made up this statistic, but it's probably correct.) Give considerable thought to what your argument should be, and talk it over with your associates. Bear in mind that in an appeal, trial counsel is not necessarily the best person to make the call. Extreme attachment to a rejected point can color one's judgment about which rulings lend themselves to effective challenge. Think of the poker player who can't bear to fold three aces even after it has come to seem very likely that the opponent has a full house.

Scattershot argument is ineffective. It gives the impression of weakness and desperation, and it insults the intelligence of the court. If you're not going to win on your stronger arguments, you surely won't win on your weaker ones. It is the skill of the lawyer to know which is which. Pick your best independent reasons why you should prevail—preferably no more than three—and develop them fully. You might contend, for example, that (1) the breach-of-contract claim is barred by the statute of limitations; (2) the performance complied with the contract; and (3) any deficiency in performance was accepted as adequate and hence waived. Of course, each point may be supported by several lines of argument.

> "We must not always burden the judge with all the arguments we have discovered, since by doing so we shall at once bore him and render him less inclined to believe us."
> —Quintilian

Lawyers notoriously multiply their points, just as they notoriously multiply their verbs ("give, grant, bargain, sell, and convey"). Some of the multifarious points often turn out to be just earlier points stated differently. Sometimes they result from including the pet theory of every lawyer on the case. Don't let that happen. Arm-wrestle, if necessary, to see whose brainchild gets cut. And don't let the client dictate your choice; you are being paid for your judgment.

On the surface, it might seem that a ten-point argument has been overanalyzed. In reality, it has been underanalyzed. Counsel has not taken the trouble to determine which arguments are strongest or endured the pain of eliminating those that are weakest.

13. Communicate clearly and concisely.

In an adversary system, it's your job to present clearly the law and the facts favoring your side of the case—it isn't the judges' job to piece the elements together from a wordy and confusing brief or argument. Quite often, judges won't take the trouble to make up for your deficiency, having neither the time nor the patience.

The judges considering your case have many other cases in hand. They are an impatient, unforgiving audience with no desire to spend more time on your case than is necessary to get the right result. Never, never waste the court's time.

> "Length dissolves vehemence, and a more forceful effect is attained where much is said in a few words.... Brevity is so useful in... style that it is often more forceful not to say something."
>
> —Demetrius

Having summoned the courage to abandon feeble arguments, do not undo your accomplishment by presenting the points you address in a confused or needlessly expansive manner. They must be presented clearly and briskly and left behind as soon as their content has been conveyed—not lingered over like a fine glass of port. Iteration and embellishment are rarely part of successful legal argument.

In a recent case before the Supreme Court of the United States, an appellant's brief took ten pages before mentioning the critical fact in the case, then took another seven pages to discuss peripheral matters before setting forth the legal rule that governed the case. No judge should have to cut through 17 pages of pulp to glimpse the core of the dispute.

Avoid the temptation to think that your brief is concise enough so long as it comes in under the page or word limit set forth in the court's rules—and more still, the temptation to insert additional material in order to reach the page or word limit. Acquire a reputation as a lawyer who often comes in short of the limits. "It's worth reading carefully what this lawyer has written," the judges think. "There's never any padding."

The power of brevity is not to be underestimated. A recent study confirms what we all know from our own experience: people tend not to start reading what they cannot readily finish.[6]

14. Always start with a statement of the main issue before fully stating the facts.

Cicero advised that you must not spring at once into the fact-specific part of your presentation, since "it forms no part of the question, and men are at first desirous to learn the very point that is to come under their judgment."[7]

In 1981, the rules of the Supreme Court of the United States were amended so that the first thing a reader sees, upon opening the cover of a brief, is the question presented. Many court rules, however, don't require issues or questions presented to be up front or even to be set forth at all. That's regrettable, because the facts one reads seem random and meaningless until one knows what they pertain to. Whether you're filing a motion in a trial court or an appellate brief—or, for that matter, an in-house memorandum analyzing some point of law—don't ever begin with a statement of facts. State the issue first.

---

6 *See* Susan Bell, *Improving Our Writing by Understanding How People Read Personally Addressed Household Mail*, 57 Clarity 40 (2007).

7 Cicero, *Cicero on Oratory and Orators* 143 (ca. 45 B.C.; Ralph A. Micken trans., 1986).

> "The greatest mistake a lawyer can make either in briefing or oral argument is to keep the court in the dark as to what the case is about until after a lengthy discussion of dates, testimony of witnesses, legal authorities, and the like. Few judges, after eventually finding out what the case is about, can back up in their mental processes and give proper consideration and evaluation to such narrative matter."
> —Hon. Luke M. McAmis

But while your statement of the issue should come before a full statement of the facts, it must contain enough of the facts to make it informative. "Whether the appellant was in total breach of contract" is a little help, but not much. Fill in the facts that narrow the issue to precisely what the court must decide: "The appellant delivered a load of stone two days late under a contract not providing that time was of the essence. Was the appellee entitled to reject the delivery and terminate the contract?"

15. Appeal not just to rules but to justice and common sense.

Courts have been known to award judgments that seem to be unjust or to defy common sense. A defective statute, or a defective Supreme Court precedent, can (in the eyes of most judges, at least) require such a result. But don't count on it. Consider the philosophy of Lord Denning, regarded by many as one of the greatest of 20th-century British judges:

> My root belief is that the proper role of a judge is to do justice between the parties before him. If there is any rule of law [that] impairs the doing of justice, then it is the province of the judge to do all he legitimately can to avoid that rule—or even to change it—so as to do justice in the instant case

26

before him. He need not wait for the legislature to intervene: because that can never be of any help in the instant case.[8]

To be sure, Denning was a renowned judicial activist— or a notorious one, if that is your view of things. But a similar, if not quite identical, approach was endorsed by the famous Chancellor James Kent of New York:

> I saw where justice lay and the moral sense decided the cause half the time, and then I sat down to search the authorities until I had exhausted my books, and I might once in a while be embarrassed by a technical rule, but *I most always found principles suited to my views of the case* ....[9]

Now you may think that the "principles" contained in the "authorities" ought to *lead* a judge to his or her conclusion, rather than merely provide later support for a conclusion arrived at by application of the judge's "moral sense." And you'd be entirely right. We're giving advice here, however, not to judges but to the lawyers who appear before them. You can bet your tasseled loafers that some judges, like Lord Denning, will be disposed to change the law to accord with their "moral sense"; and that many more will, like Chancellor Kent, base their initial decision on their "moral sense" and then scour the law for some authority to support that decision. It is therefore important to your case to demonstrate, if possible, not only that your client does prevail under applicable law but also that this result is reasonable. So you must explain why it is that what might seem unjust

---

8   Lord Denning, *The Family Story* 174 (1981).

9   *An Unpublished Letter of Chancellor James Kent*, 9 Green Bag 206, 210 (1897).

is in fact fair and equitable—in this very case, if possible—and, if not there, then in the vast majority of cases to which the rule you are urging will apply. You need to give the court a reason you should win that the judge could explain in a sentence or two to a nonlawyer friend.

Rely fully on the procedural and technical points that support your case. If, for example, a particular constitutional objection was not raised below and was not addressed by the lower court, *say so*. Whenever possible, however, accompany the procedural or technical objection with an explanation of why the pretermitted point is in any event wrong (or at least weak) *on the merits*. Judges will indeed dispose of cases on procedural or technical grounds—but they will do so much more reluctantly if it appears that the claim thereby excluded is a winner. If you cannot make a plausible case on the merits, then point out how the procedural or technical bar is necessary to ensure the correct result in the long term.

A real-life example: In a recent arbitration in Arkansas, the discovery cutoff came and went on February 15, by which time the parties had taken lengthy depositions and made voluminous production of documents. Counsel had one month left to prepare for the March 15 arbitration, which was slated to last two weeks. On March 8, the defendants issued subpoenas to four witnesses employed by the plaintiffs, requiring them to produce within five days all sorts of documents that the defendants had never before requested. The plaintiffs objected on grounds that the discovery cutoff had passed. But the arbitrators ordered the plaintiffs to produce the documents.

The result? During the week before trial (yes, in terms of the work required an arbitration is essentially a trial), while the defendants' lawyers were readying themselves—preparing their witnesses and assembling the documentary evidence—the plaintiffs' lawyers were scrambling to gather the documents required by the 11th-hour subpoenas.

The argumentative mistake? In objecting to the subpoenas, the plaintiffs' lawyers argued merely the obvious: (1) the discovery deadline had passed, and (2) the defendants could have requested these documents much earlier. The objections seemed hardly to register in the three arbitrators' minds. Here's what the plaintiffs could have—and should have—argued:

> Plaintiffs' counsel should not be forced to stop preparing for trial, one week away, and travel to four cities on both coasts to find documents that the defendants never asked for before the expired discovery deadline. There is a reason for discovery deadlines: they level the playing field. If the defendants succeed in this last-minute stratagem, the plaintiffs' team will be severely prejudiced. One week from the trial date, we should not be forced to conduct a frenetic scramble for newly subpoenaed documents. Nor should we be forced, in order to avoid that consequence, to request a deferral of the agreed-upon trial date, further delaying the justice our client is seeking. Although we are sure the defense lawyers mean well, the effect of what they have done is major-league sandbagging. We urge the panel to quash the subpoenas.

That might have worked. Certainly it stood a better chance than merely harping on the deadline. If there is prejudice, never fail to identify and argue it.

16. When you must rely on fairness to modify the strict application of the law, identify some jurisprudential maxim that supports you.

A naked appeal to fairness in the face of seemingly contrary authority isn't likely to succeed. Whenever possible, dress up the appeal with citation of some venerable legal maxim that supports your point. Such maxims are numerous, mostly derived from equity practice. For example:

> When the reason for a rule ceases, so should the rule itself.
>
> One must not change his purpose to the injury of another.
>
> He who consents to an act is not wronged by it.
>
> Acquiescence in error takes away the right of objecting to it.
>
> No one can take advantage of his own wrong.
>
> He who takes the benefit must bear the burden.
>
> The law respects form less than substance.

The State of California has codified many of these maxims with case summaries exemplifying their application.[10] Courts in other states are no less familiar with such maxims, and you can almost always find one to support a defensible position.

---

10 Cal. Civ. Code §§ 3509–3548.

17. Understand that reason is paramount with judges and that overt appeal to their emotions is resented.

It is often said that a "jury argument" will not play well to a judge. Indeed, it almost never will. The reason is rooted in the nature of what we typically think of as "jury argument"—a blatant appeal to sympathy or other emotions, as opposed to a logical application of the law to the facts. Before judges, such an appeal should be avoided.

Some authorities (though not most) defend some degree of appeal to emotions:

> Every argument . . . must be geared so as to appeal both to the emotion and to the intellect. I think the basic difference between a competent advocate and a great one is that a competent advocate can only do one or the other, or thinks only one or the other is important. You get competent advocates who are very good in emotional cases, because they are adept in appealing to the emotion. You get competent advocates who are successful in cases that are on the dry side because they have the knack of appealing to the intellect. But a great advocate is one who can appeal to both and knows how to press the two appeals in such a way that one will not get in the way of the other.[11]

We hold strongly to a contrary view:

> It is both folly and discourtesy to deliver a jury speech to [the New York Court of Appeals]. It will surely win no votes. You are fortunate if the judges will attribute such misconduct

---

11 Whitman Knapp, *Why Argue an Appeal? If So, How?*, 14 Record N.Y.C.B.A. 415, 417 (1959).

to your ignorance rather than to the vulnerability of your case.[12]

Appealing to judges' emotions is misguided because it fundamentally mistakes their motivation. Good judges pride themselves on the rationality of their rulings and the suppression of their personal proclivities, including most especially their emotions. And bad judges want to be regarded as good judges. So either way, overt appeal to emotion is likely to be regarded as an insult. ("What does this lawyer think I am, an impressionable juror?")

> "When a lawyer resorts to a jury argument on appeal, you can just see the judges sit back and give a big sigh of relief. We understand that you have to say all these things to keep your client happy, but we also understand that you know, and we know, and you know we know, that your case doesn't amount to a hill of beans, so we can go back there in the conference room and flush it with an unpublished disposition."
> —Hon. Alex Kozinski

There is a distinction between appeal to emotion and appeal to the judge's sense of justice—which, as we have said, is essential. *Of course* you should argue that your proposed rule of law produces a more just result, both in the present case and in the generality of cases. And there is also a distinction between an overt appeal to emotion and the setting forth of facts that may engage the judge's emotions uninvited. You may safely work into your statement of facts that your client is an elderly widow seeking to retain her lifelong home. But don't make an overt, passionate attempt to play upon the judicial heartstring. It can have a nasty backlash.

---

12 Simon H. Rifkind, "Appellate Courts Compared," in *Counsel on Appeal* 163, 178–79 (Arthur A. Charpentier ed., 1968).

18. Assume a posture of respectful intellectual equality with the bench.

The Solicitor General of the United States—the most frequent and often the most skilled advocate before the Supreme Court of the United States—is sometimes called the "tenth justice." Every advocate has the opportunity to deserve this description—to be so helpful to the court as to be a colleague of sorts, albeit a junior one. And that is the sort of relationship with the court, a relationship of respectful intellectual equality, that counsel should try to establish. Some appellate judges refer to oral argument as the beginning of the court's conference—an initial deliberative session in which counsel participate.

Intellectual equality requires you to know your stuff, to stand your ground, and to do so with equanimity. When you write your brief, or stand up to speak, have clearly in mind this relationship that you wish to establish. It is *not* the relationship of teacher to student—and if the judges get the impression that this is your view of things, you will have antagonized them. Nor is it the relationship of supplicant to benefactor. You are not there to cajole a favor out of the judges but to help them understand what justice demands, on the basis of your intimate knowledge of the facts and law. Perhaps the best image of the relationship you should be striving to establish is that of an experienced junior partner in your firm explaining a case to a highly intelligent senior partner.

Respect for the court is more effectively displayed by the nature of your argument (by avoiding repetition, for example, and by refraining from belaboring the obvious) than by such lawyerly obsequiousness as "if Your Honor please" or "with all due respect." Of course if you're going to err on the point, it is probably better to be unduly deferential than not deferential enough.

> "[A]n advocate should be instructive without being condescending, respectful without being obsequious, and forceful without being obnoxious."
>
> —T.W. Wakeling

19. Restrain your emotions. And don't accuse.

Don't show indignation at the shoddy treatment your client has received or at the feeble and misleading arguments raised by opposing counsel. Describing that treatment and dissecting those arguments calmly and dispassionately will affect the court quite as much. And it won't introduce into the proceeding the antagonism that judges heartily dislike. Nor will it impair your image as a reliably rational and even-tempered counselor. Ideally, you should evoke rather than display indignation.

Cultivate a tone of civility, showing that you are not blinded by passion. Don't accuse opposing counsel of chicanery or bad faith, even if there is some evidence of it. Your poker-faced public presumption must always be that an adversary has misspoken or has inadvertently erred—not that the adversary has deliberately tried to mislead the court. It's imperative. As an astute observer on the trial bench puts it: "An attack on opposing counsel undercuts the persuasive force of any legal argument. The practice is uncalled for, unpleasant, and ineffective."[13] This advice applies especially against casting in pejorative terms something that opposing counsel was fully entitled to do.

Nor should you accuse the lower court of willful distortion, even if that is obvious. A straightforward recital of the facts will arouse whatever animosity the appellate court is capable of entertaining, without detracting from the appearance of calm and equanimity that you want to project. If the court concludes that the law is against you, it will not award your client the victory just to embarrass a rogue trial judge.

20. Control the semantic playing field.

Labels are important. That's why people use euphemisms and why names are periodically changed. And that's why you should think through the terminology of your case. Use names and words that favor your side of the argument.

Consider American Airlines. Some lawyers who have represented the company call their client "AA" in briefs, perhaps as a space-saver. That passes up an opportunity for subliminal reinforcement. If American Airlines is your client, you have the opportunity to call your client "American"—knowing that every judge sitting on your case (unless you are in some international tribunal) will *be* an

---

13 Morey L. Sear, *Briefing in the United States District Court for the Eastern District of Louisiana*, 70 Tul. L. Rev. 207, 224 (1995).

American. Of course, if you're opposed to American Airlines, you will call your adversary "the Company," "the Corporation," or perhaps even "the Carrier"—never "American." If you can get your adversaries to use your terminology, so much the better.

Sometimes it's not a proper name at issue but an event. Some years ago, Warren Christopher represented Union Oil in connection with some major spills at offshore oil platforms in the Santa Barbara Channel. From the beginning, Christopher persistently referred to this potential environmental disaster as "the incident," and soon both the judge and even the plaintiffs' lawyers adopted this abstract word uniformly. Anything more concrete, from Union Oil's point of view, would have conjured up prejudicial images.

Judge James L. Robertson of Mississippi has recounted a splendid example of his use of disputational semantics when he was in practice. He was challenging some unduly restrictive outside-speaker regulations on Ole Miss's college campuses. During the proceedings, he and his partners kept referring to the lawsuit as the "speaker-ban case." Soon everyone was doing it.[14] That done, the outcome of the case seems to have been foreordained. Would you be inclined to vote for or against a speaker ban?

Of course, semantic astuteness must not degenerate into sharp practice. In a high-profile medical-malpractice action some years ago, a hospital executive named Lyman Sarnoski

---

14 Hon. James L. Robertson, "Reality on Appeal," in *Appellate Practice Manual* 119, 124–25 (Priscilla Anne Schwab ed., 1992).

(the last name is fictional) was accused of falsifying medical records. The plaintiff's lawyers repeatedly referred to him before the jury as "LIE-man," emphasizing the first syllable of his name to suggest, undoubtedly, that lying was part of his nature. It was not long before the judge ordered them to refer to the man as "Mr. Sarnoski"—and levied a $5,000 sanction on the lawyers. Even if the judge had not taken offense, the jurors probably would have.

21. Close powerfully—and say explicitly what you think the court should do.

Persuasive argument neither comes to an abrupt halt nor trails off in a grab-bag of minor points. The art of rhetoric features what is known as the peroration—the conclusion of argument, which is meant to *move* the listener to act on what the preceding argument has logically described. The concluding paragraph of a legal argument cannot, of course, be as emotional as the peroration of Cicero's first oration against Cataline. But it should perform the same function appropriately for the differing context. It should briefly call to the reader's or listener's mind the principal arguments made earlier and then describe why the rule of law established by those arguments must be vindicated—because, for example, any other disposition would leave the bar and the lower courts in uncertainty and confusion, or would facilitate fraud, or would flood the courts with frivolous litigation, and so on.

The trite phrase "for all the foregoing reasons" is hopelessly feeble. Say something forceful and vivid to sum up your points.

Legal
Reasoning

In General

22. Think syllogistically.

Leaving aside emotional appeals, persuasion is possible only because all human beings are born with a capacity for logical thought. It is something we all have in common. The most rigorous form of logic, and hence the most persuasive, is the syllogism. If you have never studied logic, you may be surprised to learn—like the man who was astounded to discover that he had been speaking prose all his life—that you have been using syllogistic reasoning all along. Argument naturally falls into this mode, whether or not you set out to make it do so. But the clearer the syllogistic progression, the better.

Legal arguments can be expressed syllogistically in two ways. Some are positive syllogisms:

> Major premise: All S is P.
> Minor premise: This case is S.
> Conclusion: This case is P.

Others are negative:

> Major premise: Only S is P.
> Minor premise: This case is not S.
> Conclusion: This case is not P.

If the major premise (the controlling rule) and the minor premise (the facts invoking that rule) are true (you must

41

establish that they're true), the conclusion follows inevitably.

Legal argument generally has three sources of major premises: a text (constitution, statute, regulation, ordinance, or contract), precedent (caselaw, etc.), and policy (i.e., consequences of the decision). Often the major premise is self-evident and acknowledged by both sides.

The minor premise, meanwhile, is derived from the facts of the case. There is much to be said for the proposition that "legal reasoning revolves mainly around the establishment of the minor premise."[16]

So if you're arguing from precedent, your argument might go:

Major premise: Our cases establish that a prisoner has a claim for harm caused by the state's deliberate indifference to serious medical needs.

Minor premise: Guards at the Andersen Unit ignored the plaintiff's complaints of acute abdominal pain for 48 hours, whereupon his appendix burst.

Conclusion: The plaintiff prisoner has a claim.

Or if you're arguing text:

Major premise: Under the Indian Commerce Clause of the U.S. Constitution, states cannot tax Indian tribes for activities on reservations without the express authorization of Congress.

Minor premise: Without congressional authorization, South Dakota has imposed its motor-fuel tax on tribes that sell fuel on reservations.

Conclusion: South Dakota's tax is unconstitutional.

---

16 O.C. Jensen, *The Nature of Legal Argument* 20 (1957).

Or if you're arguing policy:

Major premise: Only an interpretation that benefits the handicapped serves the policy objectives of the statute.

Minor premise: The defendant's interpretation of the statute requires each wheelchair-bound employee to buy additional equipment at a cost of $1,800.

Conclusion: The defendant's interpretation does not serve the policy objectives of the statute.

Figuring out the contents of a legal syllogism is a matter of finding a rule that works together with the facts of the case—really, a rule that is invoked by those facts. Typically, adversaries will be angling for different rules by emphasizing different facts. The victor will be the one who convinces decision-makers that his or her syllogism is closer to the case's center of gravity. What is this legal problem *mostly* about? Your task as an advocate is to answer that question convincingly.

> "[T]o put an argument in syllogistic form is to strip it bare for logical inspection. We can then see where its weak points must lie, if it has any."
>
> —F.C.S. Schiller

Statutes, Regulations, Ordinances, Contracts, and the Like

23. Know the rules of textual interpretation.

Paramount rule: Before coming to any conclusion about the meaning of a text, read the *entire* document, not just the particular provision at issue. The court will be seeking to give an ambiguous word or phrase meaning *in the context of the document in which it appears*. Often a later provision will reveal that the earlier provision must bear a particular meaning.

Here are the frequently expressed rules of interpretation:

- Words are presumed to bear their ordinary meanings.

- Without some contrary indication, a word or phrase is presumed to have the same meaning throughout a document.

- The provisions of a document should be interpreted in a way that renders them harmonious, not contradictory.

- If possible, no interpretation should be adopted that renders the provision in question—or any other provision—superfluous, unlawful, or invalid.

- If possible, every word should be given effect; no word should be read as surplusage.

- Legislative provisions should be interpreted in a way that avoids placing their constitutionality in doubt.

- A federal statute should not be read to eliminate state sovereign immunity or to preempt state law in an area of traditional state action unless that disposition is clearly expressed.

- Legislative provisions defining crimes and punishments will, in case of ambiguity, be given that interpretation favoring the accused (the rule of lenity).

You must also take into account the famous canons of construction. In a particular case, various canons may point in different directions. This does not prove that they are useless—only that all valid clues don't necessarily point in the same direction. It will be your job to persuade the court that most indications—from the canons and the principles of statutory construction—favor your client's interpretation. The most frequently used canons are the following:

(1) *Inclusio unius est exclusio alterius.* "The inclusion of one implies the exclusion of others." A sign that reads "open to persons 21 and over" implies that the place is *not* open to persons under 21.

(2) *Noscitur a sociis.* "A word is known by the words with which it is associated." In the phrase "staples, rivets, nails, pins, and stakes," the word "nails" obviously does not refer to fingernails.

(3) *Ejusdem generis.* "Of the same kind." A general residual category following a list of other items refers to items of the same sort. In the phrase "staples, rivets, nails, pins, stakes, and other items," the "other items" don't include balloons, but only other types of fasteners.

(4) *Ut magis valeat quam pereat.* "So that it may survive rather than perish." An ambiguous provision should be interpreted in a way that makes it valid rather than invalid.

24. In cases controlled by governing legal texts, always begin with the words of the text to establish the major premise.

As an example of textual interpretation, consider the positions that advocates might take in a case that is easy to visualize. Let's say that the Jacksons, a couple living in Santa Fe, are divorcing.[17] John is an unemployed carpenter, and his wife Jill is a successful novelist who has written five best-selling mysteries. John lays claim to half her future income on those novels, all of which were written during the marriage. Jill's attorney uncovers a curious provision in the Copyright Act:

> When an individual author's ownership of a copyright, or of any of the exclusive rights under a copyright, has not previously been transferred voluntarily by that author, no action

---

17 For much of the analysis that follows, we're indebted to Francis M. Nevins, *To Split or Not to Split: Judicial Divisibility of the Copyright Interests of Authors and Others,* 40 Fam. L.Q. 499, 513 (2006).

by any governmental body or other official or organization
purporting to seize, expropriate, transfer, or exercise rights
of ownership with respect to the copyright, or any of the
exclusive rights under the copyright, shall be given effect
under this title ....[18]

This provision becomes the major premise in Jill's attorney's syllogism:

Major premise: Section 201(e) of the Copyright Act nullifies any government's attempt to "transfer ... any of the exclusive rights" conferred by an author's copyright.

Minor premise: Treating Jill Jackson's royalties as marital property would transfer her exclusive right to those royalties conferred by her copyright.

Conclusion: Section 201(e) of the Copyright Act nullifies New Mexico's attempt to treat Jill Jackson's royalties on her books as marital property.

An excellent argument. But the debate doesn't end there.

It turns out that the only federal appellate case on point is against Jill. In *Rodrigue v. Rodrigue*, the Fifth Circuit held that the Copyright Act does not preempt state community-property doctrines.[19] The Fifth Circuit's syllogism, on which John's lawyer relies, shows the importance of reading the entire statute before interpreting one of its provisions. That syllogism was as follows:

---

18 17 U.S.C. § 201(e).

19 218 F.3d 432, 436–37 (5th Cir. 2000).

Major premise: Section 106 of the Copyright Act defines only five "exclusive rights": reproduction, adaptation, publication, performance, and display.

Minor premise: The future income stream from Jill Jackson's copyrighted works is not a right of reproduction, adaptation, publication, performance, or display.

Conclusion: The future income stream from Jill Jackson's copyrighted works is not an "exclusive right" insulated from state transfer by § 201(e).

Both sides have begun with the words of the statute, but they have crafted different arguments by emphasizing different aspects of the language—as is possible with even such a short, seemingly straightforward provision. By the way, the perceptive reader will have observed that neither Jill's syllogism nor John's takes account of the fact that § 201(e) protects not just "exclusive rights" but also "rights of ownership"—a fact that might favor Jill.

25. Be prepared to defend your interpretation by resort to legislative history.

One of your authors has described legislative history as the last surviving legal fiction in American law. The notion that the members of a house of Congress were even aware of, much less voted in reliance on, the assorted floor statements and staff-prepared committee reports that are the staple of legislative-history analysis is—not to put too fine a point on it—absurd. (And of course neither chamber could, even if it wished, *delegate* the details of a law to a committee or a floor manager.) Here again, however, we're advising not judges but the lawyers who appear before them. Since most judges use legislative history, unless you know that the judge or panel before which you are appearing does not do so, you must use legislative history as well. That is so, alas, even when the text of the statute seems entirely clear. You cannot rely on judicial statements that legislative history should never be consulted when the text is clear—not even when those statements come from opinions of the court before which you're appearing. Clarity too often turns out to be in the eye of the judicial beholder.

Conducting a thorough review of the history of major legislation is often very time-consuming, hence costly. If you have a cost-conscious client and what you consider to be an irrefutable clear-statement case, you might want to defer that task (if possible) until you see what opposing legislative history the other side comes up with. If there is nothing, it's probably a waste of time to demonstrate that the legislative history says what the statute says. But the court may not consider the text to be as crystal-clear as you do. So if money is no object, you should argue that the clarity of the text is confirmed by the legislative history.

To exemplify a legislative-history battle, let's return to the Jackson divorce case. John Jackson's attorney discovers that what triggered the enactment of § 201(e) was the Soviet Union's announcement in February 1973 that it would adhere to the Universal Copyright Convention. In literary circles, this was seen as a cunning strategy to suppress the works of Soviet dissidents, such as Alexander Solzhenitsyn, who had not yet emigrated. If the Soviets passed legislation nationalizing all overseas rights in dissidents' writings, then the Soviets could sue in the United States to enjoin publication of those "infringing" works. That is what it was all about originally. Nothing more.

The original bill, in March 1973, referred to "a foreign state or nation which purports to divest the author . . . of the United States copyright in his work."[20] In May 1975, the Copyright Office proposed extending the language to encompass any government, "including the United States or any subdivision of it."[21] And finally, before enactment, the language evolved into "any governmental body or other official or organization purporting to seize, expropriate, transfer, or exercise rights of ownership with respect to the copyright."[22] The legislative history of these revisions makes no mention of disabling a family court in a divorce case from awarding to a nonauthor spouse interests in the author spouse's copyright. And as late as 1981 only one commentator seems to have foreseen that consequence.[23]

So John Jackson's attorney argues that (1) the legislature intended to protect Soviet dissidents, not American

---

20 S. 1359, 93d Cong., 1st Sess. 58, 119 Cong. Rec. 9387 (1973).

21 Hearings on H.R. 2223 Before the Subcomm. on Courts, Civil Liberties and Admin. of Justice of the House Comm. on the Judiciary, 94th Cong., 1st Sess. 2078 (1975).

22 17 U.S.C. § 201(e).

23 See William Patry, Copyright and Community Property: The Question of Preemption, 28 Bull. of the Copyright Soc'y 237, 267 (1981).

authors seeking to deprive ex-spouses of their rightful share of marital property; (2) there is no public-policy reason to treat copyrights differently from patents or other marital property; and (3) nobody in Congress seems to have envisioned this startling result, which has more to do with the Gulag than with the Jacksons' hearth and home.

And Jill Jackson's attorney argues that (1) the words of the statute are as clear as can be; (2) the early legislative history is largely irrelevant because whatever the purpose of the original proposal, it was *purposely* broadened to include *all* governments; and (3) this broadening came at the recommendation of the Copyright Office itself.

How will the case turn out? As always, that depends on how the judges react to several factors, but especially to the gravitational pull of the differing premises. Textualists will tend to rely on the words of the statute in favor of Jill. Purposivists will probably gravitate toward John's position. Each side will try to make its premises the case's center of gravity.

Caselaw

26. Master the relative weight of precedents.

From a juridical point of view, case authorities are of two sorts: those that are governing (either directly or by implication) and those that are persuasive.

Governing authorities are more significant and should occupy more of your attention. At the appellate level, at least, the decisions most important to your case will be those rendered by the very court before which you are appearing. (That is obviously true at the court of last resort, and in intermediate appellate courts it is often the rule that one panel cannot overrule another.) The next most important body of governing decisions (the most important at the trial-court level) is that of the court immediately superior to the court before which you are appearing. It is no use arguing at length in a trial court that your point is sustained by a proper reading of a supreme-court opinion, if the intermediate appellate court to which an appeal would be taken has already rejected that reading. Of course, when the intermediate appellate court has not spoken on the point, supreme-court opinions will be the most important.

One caveat: even when the governing authority is flatly against you, if you think it is wrong you should say so, lest on appeal you be held to have waived the point. If, for example, you are appearing before a district court bound by a prior court-of-appeals precedent, it is of little use to argue at length that this precedent mistakes the law. Still, you should place in the record your view that it does so. And you should do the same in the intermediate appellate court so that there will be no doubt of your entitlement to raise that issue in the highest court of that jurisdiction.

Among the precedents that are nongoverning, there is a hierarchy of persuasiveness that far too many advocates ignore. The most persuasive nongoverning case authorities are the dicta of governing courts (quote them, but be sure to identify them as dicta) and the holdings of governing courts in analogous cases. Next are the holdings of courts of appeals coordinate to the court of appeals whose law governs your case; next, the holdings of trial courts coordinate to your court; finally (and rarely worth pursuing), the holdings of courts inferior to your court and courts of other jurisdictions.

Of the decisions rendered by these various categories of courts, the *most* persuasive within each category will be those in which the party situated like your client lost in the trial court but won reversal in the appellate court. With this kind of case, the implicit argument to the court is, "Your Honor, if you do what my adversary is asking here, you will be reversed on appeal—just as in this other case I cite." The next most persuasive decisions will be those in which the party situated like your client won in the trial court, and the appellate court affirmed. The implicit argument to the court is, "Your Honor, if you do what I am asking here, you will be affirmed on appeal—just as in this other case I cite."

If you're arguing to an appellate court, decisions of lower courts will almost never be persuasive as authority unless (1) they are numerous and virtually unanimous, or (2) the cited case was written by a judge renowned enough to be named in parentheses after the citation (e.g., Learned Hand, J.). Lengthy discussion of conflicting lower-court decisions is largely a waste of time. One should say something like this: "The decisions below are in conflict. [Compare _____ with _____.] This is a question of first impression for this court. The correct view is that taken by _____."

Another consideration for citations is freshness. In some rare situations, the older citation will be the better one. A constitutional-law opinion by Joseph Story on circuit, for example, might be more persuasive than a more recent opinion of a federal court of appeals. But at least where opinions of governing courts are concerned, the more recent the citation the better. The judge wants to know whether the judgment you seek will be affirmed by the current court, not whether it would have been affirmed 30 years ago.

When you rely on nothing but persuasive authority, it is more important than ever to say why the rule you're promoting makes policy sense. For example:

> The plaintiff's being underage tolls the statute of limitations. Though the supreme court has not had occasion to hold to this effect, it clearly expressed that view in [cite] (dictum). Minority is similar to other grounds of disability to which tolling is applied in this jurisdiction. See [cites]. And it is

uniformly held to toll the statute in our sister states. [cites]
Any other rule would result in unfairness to those unable to
protect their own interests. [Etc.]

27. Try to find an explicit statement of your major premise in governing or persuasive cases.

It is often quite easy to find a governing case with a passage that says precisely what you want your major premise to be. Say you're defending a municipality against a § 1983 suit alleging unconstitutional racial discrimination. The facts of your case, while showing some racially disparate effects of the practice in question, are entirely devoid of any indication—or even allegation—of intent to discriminate. Your syllogism might begin with this major premise:

> For violation of the Equal Protection Clause, "[a] purpose to discriminate must be present." *Washington v. Davis*, 426 U. S. 229, 239 (1976) (quoting *Akins v. Texas*, 325 U.S. 398, 403 (1945)).

When direct quotation is not possible, set forth the major premise in your own words, supported by citation of a case from a governing court. That case must clearly *hold* to that precise effect. In the example just given, if the quoted language from *Washington v. Davis* did not exist, you might argue:

> To prove a violation of the Equal Protection Clause, the plaintiff must show intentional discrimination. *Washington v. Davis*, 426 U. S. 229, 239 (1976).

Briefing

Introduction

28. Appreciate the objective of a brief.

The overarching objective of a brief is to make the court's job easier. Every other consideration is subordinate. What achieves that objective? Brevity. Simple, straightforward English. Clear identification of the issues. A reliable statement of the facts. Informative section headings. Quick access to the controlling text. In the following sections, we recommend and discuss these and other means of helping the court. But whenever you are convinced that departing from any of our recommendations, or from any convention, will make the court's job easier, depart.

Bear in mind that a good brief cannot be merely a cobbling together of separate sections and arguments but must form a coherent whole. Design the entire writing—from the statement of questions presented to the conclusion—to bring out your theory of the case and your principal themes. What two or three or four points are most important for the judge to take away? Ensure that both the structure of the brief and the content of its individual parts are designed to make these points stand out. Your purpose is to bring the court to a certain destination; the brief should be designed and built to get there.

Many briefs, particularly at the trial level, deal with subordinate issues such as standing, admissibility of evidence, and qualification of experts. You should use even these briefs to ensure, unobtrusively, that the court grasps your theory of the case as a whole. Take every available occasion to shape how the judge views your case, placing the subject of the motion being briefed in the larger context of the lawsuit and fixing in the judge's mind ideas that may help you later on.

Preparatory Steps

29. Strengthen your command of written English.

You would have no confidence in a carpenter whose tools were dull and rusty. Lawyers possess only one tool to convey their thoughts: language. They must acquire and hone the finest, most effective version of that tool available. They must love words and use them exactly.

Cultivate precise, grammatically accurate English; develop an appealing prose style; acquire a broad vocabulary. Naturally, these are not tasks you can undertake a month before your brief is due. They are lifelong projects, and you may as well begin them at once. You'll find that it's a pleasant set of tasks because the first and principal step is to read lots of good prose.

As you read, so will you write. If you read nothing but pulp novels and tabloid newspapers, you will write like them. Most lawyers have probably not descended to that level of recreational reading material—but alas, their everyday professional, nonrecreational reading is (literarily speaking) even worse. Lawyers tend to be bad writers because their profession condemns them to a diet of bad reading material. The very highest they go up the literary ladder, so to speak,

> "[C]ultivate the love of words. It is important to cultivate words, to select the right words, to put them in the right order, to know something of their meaning, of their association, of their sound."
> —Rt. Hon. Lord Birkett

is judicial opinions—which are widely read not, heaven knows, because they are well written (nor even because they are necessarily well reasoned) but because they are authoritative.

Judge Frank Easterbrook of the Seventh Circuit puts the point bluntly: "The best way to become a good legal writer is to spend more time reading good prose. And legal prose ain't that! So read *good* prose. And then when you come back and start writing legal documents, see if you can write your document like a good article in *The Atlantic*, addressing a generalist audience. That's how you do it: get your nose out of the lawbooks and go read some more."[24]

The second step in developing a good writing style is to write, and to write often. The lawyer who rarely puts pen to paper (or fingers to keyboard) will not write well. Seek out opportunities for writing not just briefs but also essays for bar journals, op-ed pieces, encomiums for departing colleagues, letters to friends—whatever will get you into the habit of converting thought into clear prose.

Meanwhile, you would do yourself an enormous favor by reading and consulting some books on English grammar and usage. That shouldn't be a dreary task if you choose good resources. Try, at the outset, Patricia T. O'Conner's *Woe Is I* (2d ed. 2004)—a delightful, highly informative guide to the pressure points of the English language. If you really want to hone your skills, read Norman Lewis's classic book *Better English* (1956), which is full of interesting exer-

---

24 Video interview with B. Garner, 20 Apr. 2006.

cises with which you can test your skills. And, of course, the classic rulebook by William Strunk and E.B. White, *The Elements of Style* (4th ed. 2000), is worth reading and rereading.

And then you'll need good desk references on English usage. Many lawyers don't even know that usage guides exist. But they do, and the best ones are wonderfully informative. Essentially, a usage guide is a compilation of literary rulings on common language questions: What's the difference between *consist of* and *consist in*? (*Consist of* introduces material things, while *consist in* introduces ideas.) What's the proper use of *begging the question*? (It means circular reasoning—assuming as true the very thing in dispute. It does *not* mean *raising the further question* or *ignoring the question*.) Should a comma appear before the *and* that introduces the final item in a series? (Preferably, yes.) Is it true that *between* refers to two things, and *among* to more than two? (No: *between* expresses reciprocal relations for any number of things, while *among* expresses a looser type of aggregate relation.) Is it all right to begin a sentence with *And* or *But*? (Yes—not only is it all right, but often it's highly desirable.) Is it all right to write *alright*? (No.) Is it proper to end a sentence with a preposition? (Yes, and it always has been.) And so on.

Our all-time favorite reference for English usage is H.W. Fowler's *Modern English Usage* (2d ed. 1965), which gives classic answers to every major question of English usage. Get the second edition as revised by Sir Ernest Gowers—

not the third edition (which in our view doesn't measure up). The largest and most current guide to American usage is the book one of us wrote: *Garner's Modern American Usage* (2d ed. 2003). It's very much in the Fowlerian mode, and it illustrates and corrects hundreds of mistakes that have crept into English since Fowler's day. Specifically for legal contexts, Garner's *Dictionary of Modern Legal Usage* (2d ed. 1995) answers thousands of questions about legal words and phrases, and their best uses.

Sometimes good writers find themselves struggling for a word that says what they want to express more precisely, or that has a more desirable tone or connotation—what we would call (but you should not call in your brief, because it is too pretentious) *le mot juste*. For this purpose, an indispensable reference book is a thesaurus, which gives synonyms for everything. The oldest and most commonly used is *Roget's Thesaurus* (available in many editions and many formats). It should be on your shelf and should soon be dog-eared. The website www.thesaurus.com is also excellent. Use these sources to find the right word, not to enable you to use multiple words for the same concept, avoiding repetition at the expense of clarity.

30. Consult the applicable rules of court.

Different courts have different rules—specifying the dates when briefs are due, the subject headings they must contain, the typefaces and type sizes in which they must be set, the maximum number of words or pages they may contain, the number of copies that must be submitted, and the manner in which they are to be filed and served. Before you even begin composing, be certain that you'll comply with the rules of the court in which you're filing. If any of them seem unclear, call the clerk of court.

Follow the rules sensibly. Occasionally lawyers interpret court rules rather perversely. Take, for example, a rule that states: "The party appealing shall be denominated the appellant, and the party against whom the appeal is taken shall be denominated the appellee." Some lawyers believe this means that they must use the terms *Appellant* and *Appellee* throughout the brief, when in fact it simply means that the style of the case (the caption on page one) should say "Joseph Jones, Appellant v. Sally Jeffers, Appellee." Call the parties Jones and Jeffers throughout if you can (see § 46); that way, you won't strip the prose of human interest.

Or let's say that a court rule specifies the following parts of a brief, in this order: procedural history, statement of facts, argument, conclusion. You're going to have to include those parts, but there's an urgent need to do something more: state the issues before you launch into the procedural history (see § 14). Check with the clerk of court to see whether the parts listed in the rule must be exclusive or whether (as you hope) you might preface those parts with "Questions Presented," or perhaps an "Introduction" or "Preliminary Statement" in which you state the issues and sum up your core points.

Now it's true that some court clerks are petty tyrants who will reject briefs that in any respect go beyond what the rules require. But our experience is that they are the exception. Call ahead to ask whether you can include an "Introduction" and perhaps even a "Table of Contents" in your brief.

31. Set timelines for the stages of your work.

There are various stages of writing: developing and gathering ideas; ordering them in an outline; drafting the text; letting the text cool; revising the text; and editing and re-editing the final product. If the only deadline you set for yourself is the filing date, you will not give each of these stages the time it deserves. Establish a schedule for completing each stage.

Let's say it's Wednesday now, and you have a brief due to be filed next Wednesday afternoon. You have to establish intermediate deadlines, and you must work backward from the filing date to set them. You'll want a clean, full draft first thing Monday morning so that you'll have time to show the brief to colleagues, amplify or trim back the ideas here and there, vet the citations, and generally polish the brief. That means you'll probably want to write the brief Saturday afternoon. (Ideally, the first draft of a brief is written in as few sittings as possible.) That means you'll want an outline by Saturday at noon (you're planning to use Sunday as a cooling-off period). And that means that you'll be preparing your outline in earnest late Saturday morning, from 11 o'clock, say, until noon. And that, in turn, means that you have until 11 a.m. Saturday to master the file, read and analyze the cases, take notes, and ponder the problem. Hence your intermediate deadlines:

> Wednesday through Saturday a.m.: research; take copious notes; brainstorm the questions presented.
>
> Late Saturday morning: prepare an outline consisting of complete sentences (the beginning of your argumentative headings).
>
> Saturday afternoon: sit down to write, blocking out all interruptions as best you can; flesh out the brief using the skeletal headings that you've already devised.
>
> Monday: revise, preferably with the help of others; prepare the table of authorities and the table of contents.
>
> Tuesday: polish; verify all citations; edit and re-edit; verify all page references in the tables.

The process we've just outlined may sound mechanistic, but it works. You'll find that you become much more efficient as a writer if you habitually establish similar benchmarks. Of course, the process is collapsible to an hour or expandable to a yearlong writing project. In fact, it pretty well describes the way we've written this book.

32. In cooperation with your opponent, prepare the Joint Appendix.

The rules of most appellate courts provide for the filing of a Joint Appendix, which contains those parts of the record on which the parties intend to rely. In the Supreme Court of the United States, this must contain (1) the relevant docket entries in the courts below, (2) any relevant pleadings, jury instructions, findings, conclusions, or opinions, (3) the judgment, order, or decision under review, and (4) any other parts of the record that the parties particularly wish to bring to the Court's attention.[25]

You obviously can't know with complete certainty what you want included in the Joint Appendix until you know what your arguments will be, and you can't be sure of that until your brief is finished. If your court, like the Supreme Court of the United States, permits the parties to request deferral of the Joint Appendix until after the briefs are filed, take advantage of that option. If that is not possible, be overinclusive rather than underinclusive.

---

25 Sup. Ct. R. 26.

The Writing Process

33. Spend plenty of time simply "getting" your arguments.

Good briefing is the product of lengthy thought. The raw material for that deliberation is the facts of your case as you contend them to be or as they have already been conceded or determined. Each one of those facts may be the basis for a legal claim or defense, or the means of establishing or defeating the relevance of governing cases. Review them in detail and prepare a timeline—a chronological listing—of the pertinent ones that must be included in your Statement of Facts.

Don't start writing until you've turned the case over in your mind for days—thinking about it while you're driving to work, discussing it with other lawyers in your firm, even talking it over with friends and family. New ideas may occur to you as you read the leading cases and scholarly authorities.

> "[T]here can be said to be three kinds of author. Firstly, there are those who write without thinking. They write from memory, from reminiscence, or even directly from other people's books. This class is the most numerous. Secondly, there are those who think while writing. They think in order to write. Very common. Thirdly, there are those who have thought before they started writing. They write simply because they have thought. Rare."
>
> —Arthur Schopenhauer

And think not just about your affirmative case but also about the case you can expect from your adversary and the responses you have available.

Don't produce a first draft too soon. That tends to freeze the deliberative process, closing off alternative approaches that ought to have been explored. Jot down new ideas as they occur to you, but don't begin writing or even outlining your brief until you have fully exhausted the deliberative process.

34. Outline your brief.

It's essential to prepare an outline before you begin to write. Eliminating this step is false economy. The time you save will be more than counterbalanced by the time consumed in deletions and revisions that will be required if you charge ahead with no plan in mind.

> "[N]o journey can be attempted before we know to what place, and by what road, we have to go."
> —Quintilian

The most satisfactory form of outline sets forth each point in a full sentence, rather than merely suggesting it by a key word. The full-sentence format has three advantages: (1) it helps you understand your own organization at a glance; (2) it often flushes out redundancies, weak links, and inconsistencies; and (3) once you've completed it, it allows you to feel as though the brief is halfway written.

At this outline stage, you will jettison the weakest arguments. If the call is a close one, you may decide to defer the cut until you've seen the argument fully fleshed out.

Opening Brief

If yours is the opening brief, the points in your outline should follow the order of argumentation described earlier: strongest point first, unless logic demands otherwise, etc. At the end of each of those separate points, refute the counter-argument that you think your adversary will bring forward. Don't put your refutation in a single section, requiring you (and the judge) to recall each of your arguments in turn.

Responding Brief

If your brief is filed second, begin by "clearing the underbrush"—responding to your opponent's seemingly persuasive points that would entirely bypass your principal point—for example, a persuasive claim of waiver or lack of jurisdiction. Then proceed in the order normal for an opening brief. But use some judgment. If your adversary's points are visibly weak—if they are unlikely to have closed the judge's mind to your principal point—answer them later.

There is, truth to tell, a division of informed opinion about the organization of a responsive brief. Some think an appellee should arrange points just as the appellant did, i.e., without regard to preliminary refutation. We stick with Aristotle, who urged a quick demolition at the outset whenever possible (see § 9). We've too often seen a judge flip back to the end of the appellee's brief, looking to see whether there is any refutation of the appellant's point that, if true—as it seemed to be—would make the appellee's first point utterly academic.

Informed opinion is also divided about the desirability—with or without preliminary refutation—of following the basic order of argument used in the appellant's brief rather than developing one's own. There is something to be said for that approach. Most judges will have read the opening brief first, and the arguments will be better engaged, and easier to follow, if they both proceed in the same order. But generally speaking, we think that benefit is outweighed by (1) the prospect (often materialized) that the organization of the appellant's brief will be a mess, and (2) the desirability of imposing your own perspective on things, placing your stronger points first and stamping your own order upon the case. Ignoring the appellant's order of battle also enables you to prepare most of your outline and brief before the opening brief is filed. You don't need to know what it contains, except for crafting responses to the few unanticipated points it raises. But again, don't be rigid. Clarity is improved by having both briefs proceed in the same order, and if there's not that much difference between your adversary's arrangement and your own preference, use the same order.

Whatever approach you take, don't allow the outline of your responsive brief to be put into final form until you've seen the appellant's brief. That is precisely why court rules give the appellee considerable time after the filing of the appellant's brief (in the Supreme Court of the United States it is 30 days)[26] instead of requiring simultaneous filing. That's more than enough time to reorder the outline and

---

26 Sup. Ct. R. 25(2).

(if you have already written your brief) to reorder sections and revise transitional passages.

Reply Brief

The reply brief is a different animal from the appellee's brief. It is not a principal brief, which is expected to make the initial presentation of important points. It is designed, as its name indicates, to reply to—to answer—points already made in an earlier brief. Some think this means that it must be devoted exclusively to (1) treating any new issues raised by the appellee's brief, and (2) answering the appellee's attacks on the appellant's principal brief. In this view, the reply brief should not reiterate or reinforce the arguments made in your principal brief, except by way of responding to the appellee's attacks. We think otherwise, for two reasons.

> "The reply should not attempt to deal with every conceivable error or omission in the appellee's brief which appellant is in a position to criticize. Nothing is more boring and less persuasive than a page-by-page, or point-by-point, attempt to rebut every inaccuracy, no matter how inconsequential. The reply should concentrate on what is significant."
> —Robert L. Stern

First, it is always desirable to place your arguments—even responsive arguments—in your own setting of the case. A mere response to the appellee's argument without any description of your own case fails to do this.

Second, and more importantly, the reply is ideally a wholly self-contained document, comprehensible without any reference to earlier writings. Why? Because many judges and law clerks have developed the habit of reading briefs in reverse order: reply first, then the responding brief, then the appellant's initial brief. That doesn't square with the expectations of counsel, who write their briefs to be read forward rather than backward. But you have to deal with the real world, which includes many retro-readers. Assume that the judge has only your reply brief in hand. Don't send the judge to your adversary's brief to understand what the case is about.

The advantage of placing your reply in the setting of your own case presentation, plus the necessity of making your reply brief comprehensible to the retro-reader, suggests that you must encapsulate your case in the reply. Since there are probably more forward-readers than retro-readers, we adhere to Aristotle's view that if your adversary has made any really telling points, you should refute them at the outset. Otherwise, begin with a quick summary of your own case, and then demonstrate the inadequacy of your opponent's response.

One thing, however, the reply brief must not contain: brand-new arguments that you didn't think of or didn't have space for in your principal brief. Raising new material that cannot be responded to is an unfair tactic that may (and should) alienate the court. When you have recapped your case, and replied to new issues and attacks contained in the appellee's brief, come to a close. Oh, and one last thing: If the appellee has raised no new issues and made no attacks that you haven't foreseen and answered in your principal brief, forgo the reply. The court doesn't want to hear you repeat yourself.

Petition for Discretionary Review

Some special considerations may apply if your brief is in support of a petition for discretionary review—commonly, though not universally, called a petition for certiorari (or cert petition). Some jurisdictions purport to grant all such petitions in which there is a substantial possibility of error below. If that is the announced policy of your jurisdiction (and if you believe it), your brief, like a merits brief on appeal, should simply seek to persuade the court that the judgment below is wrong.

But some courts as a matter of policy, and others as a matter of practice (whatever their policy states), generally limit discretionary appeals to cases raising significant issues of law—issues that deserve to be addressed by the highest court or on which the lower courts have disagreed. For example, Rule 10 of the Supreme Court of the United States provides as follows:

> Review on a writ of certiorari is not a matter of right, but of judicial discretion. A petition for a writ of certiorari will be granted only for compelling reasons. The following, although neither controlling nor fully measuring the Court's discretion, indicate the character of the reasons the Court considers:
>
> (a) a United States court of appeals has entered a decision in conflict with the decision of another United States court of appeals on the same important matter; has decided an important federal question in a way that

conflicts with a decision by a state court of last resort; or has so far departed from the accepted and usual course of judicial proceedings, or sanctioned such a departure by a lower court, as to call for an exercise of this Court's supervisory power;

(b) a state court of last resort has decided an important federal question in a way that conflicts with the decision of another state court of last resort or of a United States court of appeals;

(c) a state court or a United States court of appeals has decided an important question of federal law that has not been, but should be, settled by this Court, or has decided an important federal question in a way that conflicts with relevant decisions of this Court.

A petition for a writ of certiorari is rarely granted when the asserted error consists of erroneous factual findings or the misapplication of a properly stated rule of law.[27]

When you are confronted with a certiorari policy of this sort, it is utterly inadequate merely to show that the decision below is wrong. That might suffice in a very rare case, but not ordinarily. Indeed, not only is error not ordinarily a *sufficient* condition, it is not even a *necessary* one. A court of last resort will frequently grant review in a case that it believes has been decided correctly. It is interested in providing needed clarification of the law, and that can be done just as well by affirming the correct rule as by reversing the incorrect one.

To have a significant chance of success, you must show that the error you complain of consisted in the adoption of

---

27 Sup. Ct. R. 10.

an erroneous rule of law, not merely the erroneous application of a rule correctly expressed. It must, moreover, be
an important rule of law, not an insignificant one. Even
then, your chances are pretty slim unless you can further
show that other inferior courts in the same jurisdiction have
applied the rule of law for which you argue.

Your outline should zero in, therefore, on *these* issues,
rather than on the merits of your position. There will be
time enough to argue the merits
in great detail if discretionary
review is granted. Your first task
is to get in the door. Of course,
the merits of the case must be
argued to some extent, but not
nearly in the depth that would
be expected in a merits brief. And if none of the normal
certiorari factors are in your favor, you may have to take a
shot at getting certiorari granted simply because the case
was *so wrong*. But that is normally a very long shot indeed,
rarely worth your client's expense.

> "Lawyers might be well advised, in preparing petitions for certiorari, to spend a little less time discussing the merits of their cases and a little more time demonstrating why it is important that the Court should hear them."
> —Hon. Fred M. Vinson

Another factor distinctive to petitions for certiorari is
that judges don't like to spend a lot of time deciding what
to decide. Indeed, in most courts they won't even read the
brief in support of your petition but will rely on summaries
(or on the selection of particular briefs) by law clerks. And
law clerks don't like to spend much time on this job either.
It is all the more necessary, therefore, that your brief be
concise and utterly clear.

So it's doubly important in a petition for certiorari to limit the issues. Some courts (the Supreme Court of the United States among them) can limit the grant of certiorari to particular issues. Such a court will rarely go into those issues that are not independently certworthy simply because one certworthy issue is present. And it will surely not take a bunch of them. The noncertworthy issues simply waste the court's time and muddy the waters. It's foolish to try to piggyback onto a meritorious cert petition more than one noncertworthy issue—and the error in that one should be abundantly clear.

If you're dealing with a certiorari court that takes cases to resolve lower-court conflicts on points of law, and not to revise erroneous judgments, you must exclude prior issues that might make it impossible to *reach* the rule of law on which there is conflict. Of course, you shouldn't introduce those issues on your own—for example, by attaching to a certworthy constitutional issue an appeal from the lower court's ruling on a noncertworthy statute-of-limitations point. Since constitutional issues should not be reached unnecessarily, if the court granted certiorari on both points it would have to consider the statute-of-limitations point first—and if it found for you on that, it would never reach the certworthy issue. It is unlikely to want to do that. If it had the power to cherry-pick issues, it could simply deny certiorari on the statute-of-limitations point and grant only the constitutional issue. Again, bear in mind that courts don't like to spend a lot of time deciding what to decide. If it seems fairly certain that review of the statute-of-limitations point will not be granted, leave it out.

Some prior issues, however, cannot be avoided—such as those relating to jurisdiction and those that the respondent will raise to sustain the judgment. Sometimes the cert-worthy issue is presented only if another (noncertworthy) finding or holding of the lower court is first overturned. It is of major importance for the petitioner to lay to rest in its brief any doubts about the existence of such trouble-some prior issues. And it is of major importance for the respondent to point out that there are these hairy and insignificant issues that the court would have to deal with before it reached (if it ever could reach) the certworthy issue in the case.

Response to a Petition for Discretionary Review

A brief in opposition to a petition for discretionary review is as different from a merits respondent's brief as a brief in support of a petition for review is different from a merits petitioner's brief. Unless the only basis for the petition is that the decision below was wrong, you should focus not so much on the merits of the case as on the reasons why the usual standards for certiorari are not met. You want to argue as follows: The dispute is essentially about nothing more than a fact-finding. All other courts in the jurisdiction have expressed the same rule of law, or at least have not contradicted it. Other issues on which the petitioner has not sought certiorari suffice to sustain the judgment.

There are antecedent issues that will consume the court's time and may well prevent it from reaching the certworthy issue. Et cetera.

35. Sit down and write. Then revise. Then revise again. Finally, revise.

Any author will tell you that the hardest part of writing is getting started. Force yourself to write according to the schedule you have established.

Write the questions presented first, the body of your argument next, and then the statement of facts. Save the introduction and conclusion for later, since they usually preview and review the argument. Last of all, write the summary of the argument. Summarizing sharpens your focus—and you may well find yourself modifying the text as you summarize it. Many judges find the summary of the argument the single most important part of a brief, so don't omit this part—and give it the attention it deserves.

For the careful writer, the hardest thing after starting is stopping. Every read-through uncovers some needed change, and the job is never really done until the copy is wrested from the diligent author's grasp and sent off to the printer. Don't do all your revising on the computer. Some failings—for example, a missing connection in argument or undue length—are more easily spotted in hard copy. At least one set of edits should be made on the printed page, pen in hand.

It's helpful to lay the draft aside for a time—perhaps a few days—between read-throughs. Distance often improves the writer's perspective. This means that the time you set aside for writing the brief should be ample.

If you have the time and the friends, get some good lawyer who is not intimately familiar with the case—one who knows as much about the facts and the relevant law as the judge who will read your brief—to give the brief a quick read, about as quick as the judge's will be. A reader off the street, so to speak, will sometimes be able to spot gaps and deficiencies that you are too close to the argument to perceive.

> "Undoubtedly ... the best method for correction is to lay by for a time what we have written, so that we may return to it after an interval as if it were something new to us, and written by another, lest our writings like newborn infants compel us to fix our affections on them."
> —Quintilian

The next-to-last read-through should be devoted solely to compression—eliminating those sentences, phrases, and words that do no work. Every word that is not a help is a hindrance because it distracts. A judge who realizes that a brief is wordy will skim it; one who finds a brief terse and concise will read every word. The final read-through should be exclusively devoted to seeing whether certain points can be put more clearly, more vividly, more crisply.

Architecture and Strategy

36. Know how to use and arrange the parts of a brief.

Be sure to include all parts of the brief required for the court in which your brief will be filed. For this purpose, you may need to consult both generally applicable provisions (e.g., Federal Rule of Appellate Procedure 28) and the rules of the particular court (see § 30). Since some sections of a brief are highly desirable even when not required, you may have to find out (ordinarily from the clerk of court) what additions to the requirements are permitted.

There is considerable variety in briefing requirements, even among courts at the same level. Two intermediate appellate courts, for example, may have quite different local rules. The difference is particularly marked, however, between appellate courts and trial courts in general. The required parts of briefs in the latter are typically many fewer. (So the Federal Rules of Civil Procedure, unlike the Federal Rules of Appellate Procedure, contain no briefing requirements.) This is understandable, since briefs at the trial level include not just posttrial briefs, which may approximate appellate briefs, but also many briefs on various filings, such as a motion for summary judgment, a motion to exclude evidence, etc.

In the discussion below, we have marked with daggers those sections that should be included in all trial-court briefs. We have marked with asterisks those sections that should ideally be included in all appellate briefs and in trial-court briefs that perform a similar function.

†*Questions Presented

As we've noted, the rules of the Supreme Court of the United States require what virtually no other court rules require: that the questions presented for review be set forth on the first page of the brief, in splendid isolation from all other material. On opening the brief, the Questions Presented are the first things the Justices see.

Unless the rules of your court forbid this practice (and we know of none that do), follow it religiously—even in memoranda in support of motions. Place right up front what it is you want the judges to resolve. This may well be the most important part of your brief.

A noted lawyer—who, exactly, is unclear because the quotation is variously attributed to Rufus Choate, Clarence Darrow, John W. Davis, and others—said that he would gladly take either side of any case as long as he could pick the issues. Many advocates fail to appreciate that the outcome of a case rests on what the court understands to be the issue the case presents. You want to state the issue fairly, to be sure, but also in a way that supports your theory of the case. A well-framed issue statement suggests the outcome you desire.

> "[I]n every sense of the word—and in all seriousness—it can be said that the most important paragraph in a brief is the first one, in which appears counsel's formulation of the issues presented for decision."
>
> —Frank E. Cooper

Take *Eisenstadt v. Baird,* in which the plaintiffs attacked a state law that prohibited the sale of contraceptives to unmarried people. Here is how the Supreme Court framed its conclusion:

> If the right of privacy means anything, it is the right of the *individual,* married or single, to be free from unwarranted governmental intrusion into matters so fundamentally affecting a person as the decision whether to bear or beget a child.[28]

The question it was addressing, the issue it had framed, was whether the right of privacy means that. Judge Richard A. Posner of the Seventh Circuit has observed that the decision might not have seemed so clear-cut if the Court hadn't "set up a straw man"[29]—if, instead, the Court had posed the issue as follows:

> We must decide whether the state is constitutionally obligated to allow the sale of goods that facilitate fornication and adultery by making those practices less costly.[30]

As an advocate, you want to find the premise that will pull the court toward your conclusion and then make that premise explicit in your statement of the issue. If the court decides to answer the question you pose, it will probably reach the conclusion you urge.

Never forget, however, that you are here to reason with the court and cannot do so successfully if you show your-

---

28 405 U.S. 438, 453 (1972) (emphasis in original).

29 Richard A. Posner, *Law and Literature: A Misunderstood Relation* 305 (1988).

30 Adapted from *id.*

self to be unreasonable. The very first display of irrationality likely to come to the court's attention is your manner of framing the issue presented. Make it honest and fair. Show enough respect for the intelligence of the court not to include irrelevancies. Never color the issue with loaded adjectives and argumentative consequences—as by saying that the issue is "Whether the appellee could bring this suit a long 15 years after the claim arose, risking the loss or disappearance of witnesses and evidence necessary for the defense?" Any 15 years is a long 15 years. The loss of witnesses and the loss of evidence are reasons why the applicable statute of limitations should be enforced and are perhaps relevant factors in determining whether the longer or the shorter of two potentially applicable statutes applies. But those points belong in argument. They form no part of the issue presented. You know it, the court knows it, and you lose credibility by pretending otherwise.

The most persuasive form of an issue statement—the so-called deep issue[31]—contains within it the syllogism that produces your desired conclusion (see § 22). Consider the case of *Rousseve v. Jones*,[32] decided in 1997 by the Supreme Court of Louisiana. Rousseve had paid five years' worth of child support to his former wife for his daughter Aleigha. But then biological testing proved that Aleigha was not his daughter after all. So he sought reimbursement from Aleigha's mother for the money he'd paid over the years

---

31 *See* Garner, *The Winning Brief* 53–97 (2d ed. 2004).
32 704 So. 2d 229 (La. 1997).

under the false impression that he was the father. His syllogism had some appeal:

> Major premise: Under Louisiana law, a husband who is not the father of his wife's child is not obliged to pay support for that child.
>
> Minor premise: Blood tests have conclusively shown that Rousseve is not Aleigha's father.
>
> Conclusion: Rousseve was not obliged to support Aleigha (and he is entitled to reimbursement for his payments).

Jones, the ex-wife, had a syllogism of her own:

> Major premise: Under Louisiana law, a husband is presumed to be the father of his wife's child unless he denies paternity within one year of the child's birth.
>
> Minor premise: Rousseve did not deny paternity within one year of Aleigha's birth.
>
> Conclusion: Rousseve was presumed to be the father of Aleigha during the five years in question.

In the end, the Louisiana Supreme Court agreed with the ex-wife. But let's consider how that case could have been effectively presented, syllogistically, in the issue statement. It would have been all but pointless to state the issue abstractly: "Whether Rousseve is entitled to reimbursement paid during the first five years of Aleigha's life?" Only the other parts of the brief might enlighten the reader. See what happens, however, if the ex-wife's syllogism is collapsed into a three-sentence question presented:

> Under Louisiana law, a husband is presumed to be the father of his wife's child and must support the child unless he denies

paternity within one year of the child's birth. Rousseve did not deny paternity until five years after Aleigha's birth. Was he obliged to support Aleigha until he proved that he was not her father?

In 57 words, that issue is clean and informative.

When your major premise is completely obvious, it is possible to leave it implied. Aristotle termed the resulting statement an "enthymeme"—simply a syllogism with an implied major premise. For example:

> [Major premise (implied): A contract is not binding without
> consideration.]
> Minor premise: Johnson provided no consideration for this
> contract.
> Conclusion: This contract is not binding.

Or, to turn the enthymeme into a question:

> Given that Johnson provided no consideration for this contract, can he enforce it?

Some counsel erroneously assume that a court rule requiring the brief to contain a statement of the question presented demands a one-sentence question that contains all the relevant premises. The result is often a rambling statement that no mortal reader could wade through:

> Whether there was a violation of the OSHA rule requiring every incident-investigation report to contain a list of factors that contributed to the incident, when the investigation report on the June 2002 explosion at the Vespante plant listed the contributing factors in an attachment to the report entitled "Contributing Factors," as opposed to including them in the body of the report?

That's a muddle. We forget the question by the time we reach the question mark. One reason is that the time is out of joint: we first get a word posing a present interrogative (*whether*), then back up to what happened, and then, with the question mark, have to jump back to the present.

The better strategy is to break up the question into separate sentences totaling no more than 75 words. The first sentences follow a chronological order, telling a story in miniature. Then, emerging inevitably from the story, the pointed question comes at the end:

> OSHA rules require every incident-investigation report to contain a list of factors that contributed to the incident. The report on the June 2002 explosion at the Vespante plant listed the contributing factors not in the body of the report but in an attachment entitled "Contributing Factors." Did the report thereby violate OSHA rules?

Instead of one 62-word sentence, we have three sentences averaging just 18 words. The information is presented in a way that even readers unfamiliar with this area of the law can easily understand.

Moreover, because seasoned legal readers are always impatient to find out what the case is about, opening a brief with the deep issue satisfies a real need. It's infinitely better than the naked, uninformative legal question: "Did the incident-investigation report on the June 2002 explosion at the Vespante plant violate OSHA rules?"

Briefing

Statement of Parties in Interest

Rule 24(1)(b) of the Supreme Court of the United States provides that a merits brief must contain a "list of all parties to the proceedings in the court whose judgment is under review" unless the caption of the case names them. Comply with any similar requirement of your court.

*Table of Contents; Table of Authorities

The Table of Contents sets forth your section headings and subheadings. It is primarily a finding tool, but it also serves a second purpose: many judges look at it first to get a quick overview of the argument. That's one reason you should make your section headings and subheadings full, informative sentences (see § 40). For the same reason, be sure to format the Table of Contents with outline-style progressive indentation displaying the hierarchy of your argument—that is, subsections indented more than sections.

The Table of Authorities is more important than you might think. Some judges will fan through it just to assess how careful a lawyer they are dealing with. Compiling the table is not a job that can be left to an unsupervised secretary. Unless the rules provide otherwise, include separate sections for (1) cases, (2) official texts (constitutional provisions, statutes, regulations, and ordinances), and (3) miscellaneous authorities. Cases should be in alphabetical order; official texts should be grouped by type and, within each type (except for constitutional provisions), should be set forth in order of enactment or adoption; miscellaneous authorities should be in alphabetical order. Citations must be in proper form. Briefs filed in the Supreme Court of the United States by the Solicitor General provide a good model; they're available online.

Never trust computers to prepare the tables automatically. And because last-minute editing of the brief may alter the pagination, always run a final check of the page references in both tables. Also, KeyCite or Shepardize the cases in the Table of Authorities. Allow a full day for all this work.

Constitutional and Statutory Authorities

The rules of the Supreme Court of the United States require the constitutional and statutory authorities involved in the case to be cited (not necessarily quoted) in a separate section of the brief.[33] It seems to us not essential to follow this practice if the rules of your court don't require it. If you do follow it, little is to be gained by quoting as well as citing the provisions in question. If they are few and concise, they are better quoted where relevant in your Argument, as they're being discussed. If they are extensive and lengthy, they are better included in an Appendix (if that's allowed).

---

33 Sup. Ct. R. 14(1)(f), 24(1)(f).

*Statement of Jurisdiction

The Federal Rules of Appellate Procedure require a statement of the basis for jurisdiction, not only of the court of appeals, but also of the district court or the agency from which appeal is taken, including citations of applicable statutory provisions and a statement of facts and filing dates establishing jurisdiction.[34] Some courts require no statement of jurisdiction whatever, but in our view it is good self-discipline (and insurance against embarrassment) to provide it: "This Court has jurisdiction under _____." If there is serious dispute or even serious doubt about whether the suit or appeal comes within that provision, this is not the point to get into it. Discuss that in the Argument section of your brief.

†Introduction or Preliminary Statement

Some court rules and customs provide for a separate Introduction or Preliminary Statement. In motion practice, where there typically is no Summary of Argument, the Introduction may be used to set forth the questions presented and the argument summary. In an appellate brief, however, if you have written a competent statement of the Questions Presented, and plan to provide a Summary of the Argument, we see little need for a separate Introduction, especially one that precedes the Statement of Facts and Proceedings Below. Perhaps the court rule can be satisfied by using the Introduction to set forth the questions

---

34 Fed. R. App. P. 28(a)(4).

presented or by titling your Summary of Argument section "Introduction and Summary of Argument," and making a brief introduction at that point.

Whatever you do, don't allow this section to duplicate what is written elsewhere. Repetition bores, and boredom invites skimming.

Proceedings Below

Some appellate courts require a separate statement of the proceedings below—a division of the brief sometimes called "Statement of the Case."[35] Under many court rules, this precedes the Statement of Facts.

That order of things is troublesome. Often the proceedings below aren't comprehensible without an understanding of some of the facts to which the proceedings pertain. The rules of the Supreme Court of the United States do not provide for such a separate division of the brief, and the proceedings below are set forth at the end of the section dealing with the facts giving rise to the controversy—that is, both the operative and the procedural facts appear in a single narrative, in the chronological order in which they occurred.

If your court rules permit you to order your brief this way—perhaps by heading your section "Statement of Facts and Proceedings Below"—you should do so.

Wherever your description of the proceedings below appears, limit it to the procedural facts, the decisions, and

---

35 Fed. R. App. P. 28(a)(6).

the reasons for decisions relevant to the matters on appeal. The court isn't interested in matters that don't affect the issues at hand, such as settlements reached on side issues and orders not germane to the appeal. Avoid needless detail. Your goal at this stage isn't to argue, but to tell the court how the issues before it arose procedurally and how the case got here.

†*Statement of Facts

In most jurisdictions, rules require a Statement of Facts soon after the introduction. (In the Supreme Court of the United States, it's called the "Statement of the Case.") It is narrative rather than argument: a description of the facts of the case and the proceedings to date, with citations of the Joint Appendix or the record. Omitting a fact crucial to your case is a critical mistake. An even worse one is misstating a fact. Nothing is easier for the other side to point out, and nothing can so significantly damage your credibility.

Although you must not misstate a fact, you need not exclude all matters that are disputed. Sometimes you must include them. A posttrial merits brief in the trial court, for example, should set forth *your* view of what happened. Just be sure you do not present it as undisputed truth. "The evidence that the plaintiff introduced showed that . . . ." Of course, if you are appealing a judgment that included findings of fact, you must accept them as true—unless one of the grounds for your appeal is that they are clearly errone-ous. If you are appealing from a grant of summary judgment, you need not show that the version of the facts your evidence established is true, but only that the evidence raises a genuine dispute about a material fact. And so forth. (The variations of proper factual allegations are so numerous that it is impossible to itemize them here.)

> "The notion that the facts, whether simple or complicated, speak for themselves is sheer nonsense. In reality, there are as many ways of telling the story of any case as there are fleas on a dog. Subtleties of arrangement and emphasis; the selection of particular words or phrases; and innumerable little twists and turns all play their significant part and are worthy of study."
> —Harold R. Medina

To say that the Statement of Facts must not contain argument is not to say that it cannot be designed to persuade. Like everything else in your brief, it *must* be. You advance that objective by your terminology, by your selection and juxtaposition of the facts, and by the degree of prominence you give to each. Rhetorically speaking, you'll be putting some facts in high relief and some in low relief—and you'll be omitting others altogether. You'll be engaging in what Aristotle called amplification and diminution. You will amplify the facts that suggest your desired outcome by placing them prominently in the narrative.

Be careful, however, about introducing sympathetic facts that are legally irrelevant. It is reasonable to humanize your tort–plaintiff client by describing her as an 80-year-old widow. It goes over the top to emphasize that her deceased husband was a county judge. The judges (the living ones reading your brief) will see through this naked play for favoritism and will think less of you because obviously you think less of them.

A fair statement of the facts includes relevant facts adverse to your case. They will come out anyway, and if you omit them you simply give opposing counsel an opportunity to show the court that you're untrustworthy. Of course, don't include damaging facts that are irrelevant—for example, the fact that the opposing party is the penniless widow of a Purple Heart recipient. Moreover, if your research has uncovered a subsidiary issue that favors the other side but that opposing counsel may not be aware of, don't flag the point by including facts that can be relevant only to that issue.

A narrative must be basically chronological. Lawyers commonly fail in this fundamental point of exposition by rehearsing a witness-by-witness account of a hearing or trial. No. A witness-by-witness account is appropriate only when the issue is evidentiary support for the trial-court judgment—and even then it should be ordered fact-by-fact, and witness-by-witness only as to each fact. In general, the way to state facts is to tell the story not of witnesses on the stand but of the events that gave rise to the legal dispute. In preparing to do this well, you'll need to produce a raw-material "chronology of events" sequencing all the facts in order by time, day by day and hour by hour.

But never begin statement after statement with dates. A few dates will be important, but for the others simply say "The next morning...," "That afternoon...," etc. Remember: if you spell out every date, you confuse the reader and bog down the story.

If your brief is responding to an opponent's brief, you will almost certainly want to set forth a full counterstatement of facts. Why? Because it's almost unimaginable that competent opposing counsel will tell the story in a way that is best for your client. If you don't tell the story your way, you'll surrender dozens of opportunities to foreshadow your legal and equitable arguments.

But making a full counterstatement presents a problem: the court may not read it. (Who wants to read the same mystery twice?) Some advise that if you want to ensure that the court will read your significant corrections to the first-filed brief, you should simply say that you agree with the appellant's statement of facts, but "with the following significant exceptions." The theory is that the court will be certain to read that. All in all, though, we think it best to make a complete counterstatement, emphasizing the most salient disagreements at the outset. This is preferable not only because of the tactical advantage of getting the story as you tell it before the court (if the court reads it), but also because you want your brief to be self-contained—a complete document to which the court can refer for all aspects of the case.

**Summary of Argument*

The rules of some courts require a Summary of Argument and don't count it against the brief's page or word limit. Other courts don't require it and subtract it from your permitted length. You should include it anyway. Write it after completing the Argument, though it precedes that section in your brief.

> "The Summary may be . . . the only part of the brief some judges will ever read, either because they find the case simple enough to decide without further study or because they are too overloaded with work, or simply unwilling to work very hard."
>
> —Robert L. Stern

Some judges never read the Summary of Argument, which will precede the Argument section of your brief. Why read a cut-down version when you're about to read the real thing? Other judges, however, consider the Summary of Argument indispensable—indeed, the most important part of the brief. As long as judges of the latter sort exist, and the judge you're appearing before has not publicly committed, you must include the Summary. Omit it only if it is not required, if it is counted against your brief limit, and if it takes up space that you absolutely require for full exposition of your points.

Unlike the Introduction, the Summary of Argument is not just a preview of the topics of argument that are to follow. It is a short version of the substance of the arguments under each topic. How short is short? In a 50-page brief, we recommend no more than five pages, and ideally no more than three. State the main lines of thought without embellishment, omit quotations, and cite only key cases (if any at all).

†*Argument

The Argument is the guts of your brief, the part for which all the rest is just preparation and summary. Two points are crucial.

First, keep your eye on the ball. Write down at the outset, and keep before you throughout your drafting of the Argument, the syllogism that wins your case. Each aspect of the Argument must be consistent with this and should be no more sweeping than necessary to support it. Nothing should be irrelevant to it.

Second, be brief. We have said it before, and (contrary to what you must do in your Argument) we will say it again: a brief that is verbose and repetitious will only be skimmed; a brief that is terse and to the point will likely be read with full attention. So a long and flabby brief, far from getting a judge to spend more time with your case, will probably have just the opposite effect.

Ponder this: Judges often associate the brevity of the brief with the quality of the lawyer. Many judges we've spoken with say that good lawyers often come in far below the page limits—and that bad lawyers almost never do.

Brevity requires ruthlessness in wringing out of your argument everything that doesn't substantially further your case: entire points that prove to be weak; paragraphs or sentences that are unnecessary elaboration; words and phrases that add nothing but length.

Brevity means abandoning string cites with more than three cases. (If you're dueling with opposing counsel about what constitutes "the weight of authority," put all your cases in a footnote.) Indeed, string cites should not be used *at all* except for propositions of law that may be novel to the court. Obvious points can be made by citing a single governing case, a statute, or even a well-known treatise: "No contract is enforceable without valid consideration. *Smith v. Jones* [citation]."

> "[W]hen judges see a lot of words they immediately think: LOSER, LOSER. You might as well write it in big bold letters on the cover of your brief."
> —Hon. Alex Kozinski

Never ask for extra pages in a brief. Never. (Well, almost never.) Hire some good editors instead.

If you're writing for a multijudge panel whose composition you know beforehand, avoid the temptation to direct your argument solely to the judge whom you expect to be the "swing" vote. Write for the whole court. Obvious pandering to the idiosyncratic views of a single judge, to the exclusion of the others, will be noticed and resented. Even if you think the rest of the panel is safely in your corner, don't let that presumptuous calculation shine forth in your brief. The same holds true, of course, for your oral presentation.

A final thought: If you represent an appellee or respondent, rely on the trial court's opinion. You may occasionally be defending a judgment on which the trial court's opinion is simply indefensible, and then you must argue for affirmance on other grounds. Ordinarily, however, the trial court did the right thing (in your estimation) for the right reason. Refer to and rely on the trial court's opinion. There are three good reasons: (1) it's persuasive because it represents the conclusion of another judge in this very case; (2) deferential treatment of the opinion below shows the appellate court that you respect the bench; and (3) you may have to appear again before that same trial judge, who will not appreciate your repudiating on appeal the goods you successfully peddled at trial.

†*Conclusion

Most court rules require, as a separate section, a conclusion—in the words of the rules of the Supreme Court of the United States, "[a] conclusion specifying with particularity the relief the party seeks."[36] Some brief-writers, including the Solicitor General of the United States, take this to permit nothing more than the request for relief ("The judgment of the court of appeals should be affirmed").

We think you should be more ambitious. You must include the request for relief, to be sure. But you can preface that with a true conclusion to your argument—one or two paragraphs encapsulating your winning syllogism in a fresh and vivid way. Try to make it more than a pro forma short regurgitation of what has preceded. It should be, so

---

36 Sup. Ct. R. 24(1)(j).

to speak, the distance runner's devastating kick at the end of the race.

Appendix

If the arguments in a case refer to many texts—for example, many related regulations that shed light on the meaning of the particular regulation in question—it's a good idea to collect these texts in an Appendix to the brief. Even if they are quoted piecemeal in your Argument section, you'll facilitate comprehension by setting them next to each other, all in one place.

You can't be sure that the judge reading your brief will lay it down to look up your reference to the Code of Federal Regulations (which may not be easily accessible anyway) or even to consult a compendium of the regulations in the Joint Appendix. Any text essential to your brief should be in your brief. Note, however, that some courts have special rules or practices involving appendixes; unless the rules clearly permit one, you should check with the clerk's office.

37. Advise the court by letter of significant authority arising after you've filed your brief.

If you don't expect an immediate ruling, you will naturally keep track of developments in the field—new legislation and new rulings from governing authorities. If a significant development supports your case—or even that of the other side—you should bring it to the attention of the court by letter, with a copy to opposing counsel.[37] The letter should concisely explain why the development supports your case, or does not substantially impair it. If oral argument has been scheduled for a later date, it is unprofessional to withhold favorable new authority and spring it on opposing counsel at that time.

Try to keep your letter to one page.

38. Learn how to use, and how to respond to, amicus briefs.

The major advantage of making or clarifying law through legislation is that in theory—and in practice, if it is done right—all interested parties can have their say. Not so with adjudication. To be sure, in principle the adjudicative judgment binds only the parties before the court. The doctrine of stare decisis, however, ensures that the legal rules necessary to the court's decision become the law for everyone within the court's jurisdiction. Thus, those who frequent the hearings of the Supreme Court of the United States are familiar with the scene in which a courtroom full of tall-building lawyers, meters running on "high," winces in pain as some trial lawyer inexpert at appellate advocacy (but lucky enough to have gotten cert granted) butchers a point of law crucial to all their clients.

The amicus brief is an increasingly popular device designed with the hope of giving these other interested parties their say. We say "with the hope" because judges rarely

---

37 *See* Fed. R. Civ. P. 28(j).

read all the amicus briefs. They will surely read one filed by the United States, probably one filed by the ACLU in a civil-rights case or by the AFL CIO in a labor-law case, and probably one filed by a lawyer in whose integrity and ability they have special confidence (yet another reason to develop a reputation for these qualities). The rest will very likely be screened by law clerks, with only a few (if any) making it to the judge's desk.

Amicus briefs pose special problems, both for the side they favor and for the side they oppose. It is difficult to generalize about them, since they serve so many different purposes. Perhaps the most common purpose, at least in courts of last resort, is to enable the officers of trade associations to show their members that they are on the ball. To achieve this end, it really does not matter what the amicus brief says. It can track the party's brief; the filing of it is what counts. The same can be said of the amicus brief filed by 35 states, or by the chief law-enforcement officers of 50 metropolitan jurisdictions. The very cover of the brief makes its principal point—a very telling point in support of a petition for discretionary review: this case involves an issue of grave national importance.

With respect to amicus briefs on your side of the case, the best advice we can give is a caveat: it is perfectly appropriate to encourage filings by amici—for example, by advising the civil division of the Justice Department or the National Association of Attorneys General that your case involves an issue in which they have a considerable stake. But it is unethical for you or your client to have any part in funding or preparing the amicus brief. You can tell an inquiring amicus what you intend to argue, but do not suggest what the amicus should argue to complement that. Coordination is the amicus's job, not yours.

What about amicus briefs on the other side of the case? You cannot afford to ignore them entirely. Significant additional points raised by a prominent amicus (the United States, for example, or the agency with responsibility for the field that the litigation involves) must be answered. Yes, it does seem unfair—rather like giving your adversary double the page limit that you have—but life is like that. You can probably afford to make no response to the other amici, unless one of them makes a seemingly persuasive argument that is fundamentally different from your adversary's approach—for example, arguing that the dispositive text has a meaning different from what your adversary claims, but one that still causes your client to lose. You should respond to this briefly on the merits, but preface the response with the protestation that the point was not raised below and is not fairly included within the question on which discretionary review was granted. As for the other amicus briefs, say nothing—but be prepared to answer at oral argument questions based upon their contents.

An increasingly popular category of amicus brief is the academic brief—"Brief on Behalf of Legal Historians," or "Brief on Behalf of Professors of Securities Law." These are usually drafted by a few professors and then circulated from law faculty to law faculty, seeking professorial sign-ups. Advocacy and scholarship do not go well together, which is why many academics never lend their names to professorial amicus briefs. Some judges, however, may give these filings undue weight. An easy way to cut them down to size is to run a literature check under the names of the signatories. You'll often find that most of them have produced no scholarly publication on the point in question or sometimes even in the field at issue. Point this out to the court. And if it is so, point out that some academic publications (by professors who remain, perhaps, too immersed in their scholarship to hustle up an advocacy brief) favor your side of the case. If the academic brief seems particularly damaging, you might take the trouble to check the scholarly writings of the signatories; some professors have been known (*O tempora, O mores!*) to join a brief that flatly contradicts their own writings. By noting this, you'll help both the court and the academy.

What if you're writing an amicus brief yourself? Don't replow the ground you expect the party you're supporting to cover—*unless* you have reason to believe that the party you're supporting is using a particularly dull plow. It sometimes happens (though rarely) that an amicus brief will do a much better job than the party's brief on the party's own basic theory of the case. Ordinarily, however, you should try to develop a "take" on the case that is different from what the party produces; or to discuss in great depth an aspect of the case (for example, historical material) that the party will not have much time for; or perhaps (if you are supporting the appellee) to defang a particular amicus brief filed on behalf of the appellant. Our constant injunction of brevity has special force here, since not even the demands of duty drive judges to read amicus briefs that are bloated. Make the one or two points (preferably one) that you think will contribute something important and new—and close.

Writing Style

39. Value clarity above all other elements of style.

In brief-writing, one feature of a good style trumps all others. Literary elegance, erudition, sophistication of expression—these and all other qualities must be sacrificed if they detract from clarity. This means, for example, that the same word should be used to refer to a particular key concept, even if elegance of style would avoid such repetition in favor of various synonyms. It means that you must abandon

> "All the careful strategy in the world will be of no assistance to you unless you write clearly and forcefully. And clarity and power are above all the fruit of simplicity."
> —Hon. Irving R. Kaufman

interesting and erudite asides if they sidetrack the drive toward the point you are making. It means that you should never use a word that the judge may have to look up. It means that nothing important to your argument should appear in a footnote.

Further, it means shunning puffed-up, legalistic language. Make your points and ask for your relief in a blunt, straightforward manner.

> Wrong: The undersigned counsel do hereby for and on behalf of their clients, for the reasons explained hereinbelow, respectfully request that this Honorable Court consider and hereby rule that no issues of material fact do exist in the instant controversy, and that a final judgment be entered in favor of the

> client of the undersigned counsel (sometimes herein referred to as "Defendant" or "Cross-Plaintiff") and against Plaintiff.
>
> Right: Johnson requests entry of summary judgment.

Clarity is amply justified on the ground that it ensures you'll be understood. But in our adversary system it performs an additional function. The clearer your arguments, the harder it will be for your opponent to mischaracterize them. Put yourself in the shoes of a lawyer confronting an opposing brief that is almost incomprehensible. You struggle to figure out what it means—and so does the court. What an opportunity to characterize the opposing argument in a way that makes it weak! This can't happen to you—your opponent will not be able to distort what you say—if you are clear.

40. Use captioned section headings.

Many court opinions dispense with captions for sections and subsections, relying on numbers and letters alone (I, II, and III; A, B, and C within each). Whatever the value of that practice in opinions (and even that is questionable), it's not a good approach for briefs. Since clarity is the all-important objective, it helps to let the reader know in advance what topic you're about to discuss. Headings are most effective if they're full sentences announcing not just the topic but your position on the topic: Not "I. Statute of Limitations" but "I. The statute of limitations was tolled while the plaintiff suffered from amnesia."

The section headings in a typical appellant's brief might read as follows:

1. The four year statute of limitations bars this action because Bartleby waited six years to file suit.
2. Two essential elements of fraud—intent to deceive and detrimental reliance—were not established.
   A. The record contains no evidence of an intent to deceive.
   B. The record contains no evidence of detrimental reliance.
3. Conclusion.

Theoretically, each of these headings could be further broken down into subheadings. Every argument, for example, could be divided into (1) major premise, (2) minor premise, (3) conclusion, and (4) refutation of opposing arguments. But such excessive subdivision clutters more than clarifies. Avoid overkill.

41. Use paragraphs intelligently; signpost your arguments.

Section headings are not the only means of mapping your argument. Within each captioned section, paragraph breaks perform the same function. The first sentences of paragraphs (your fifth-grade teacher called them "topic sentences") are as important as captioned section headings in guiding your readers through your brief—telling them what next thought is about to be discussed. Paragraph breaks should not occur randomly, inserted simply because the last paragraph was getting too long. They should occur when you are moving on to a new subpoint and wish to signal a change of topic.

One writer on brief-writing (who must remain nameless) suggests that no paragraph should be more than five sentences long. We think that's bad advice. Your readers didn't make it to the bench by reading only Classic Comics. Judges are accustomed to legal argumentation, which often—indeed, usually—requires more than five sentences to develop an idea. Use as many sentences as the thought demands. If the paragraph is becoming unusually long (say a page of your brief), break the idea into two paragraphs if possible. (¶ "Another factor leading to the same conclusion . . . .") Some ideas will take only five sentences—indeed, some may take only three. But a brief with paragraphs of rigidly uniform length is almost sure to be a bad brief. Use what it takes.

> "The topic sentence . . . smooths the way from paragraph to paragraph by binding that which has been said to that which is going to be said. By hooking the previous series of ideas to the coming one, it provides momentum."
>
> —Sherman Kent

In helping the reader follow the progression of thought—both between and within paragraphs—guiding words are essential. Consider the difference between the following two progressions: (1) "He is not a great sprinter. He came in third." (2) "He is not a great sprinter. But he came in third." The word "but" signals that the next thought will somehow qualify the point just made. Or your second sentence might have been "After all, he came in third"—the "After all" signifies that the upcoming thought will affirm the previous one. Or you might have used a subordinating conjunction: "Although he is not a great sprinter, he came in third."

There are many such guiding words and phrases: *moreover, however* (preferably not at the head of a sentence), *although, on the other hand, nonetheless, to prove the point,* etc. These words and phrases turn the reader's head, so to speak, in the direction you want the reader to look. Good writers use them abundantly.

Normally, the very best guiding words are monosyllabic conjunctions: *and, but, nor, or, so,* and *yet.* Professional writers routinely put them at the head of a sentence, and so should you. There's a myth abroad that you should never begin a sentence with a conjunction. But look at any species of reputable writing—whether it's a good newspaper, journal, novel, or nonfiction work—and you're likely to find several sentences per page beginning with one of those little connectives. You can hardly achieve a flowing narrative or argument without them.

42. To clarify abstract concepts, give examples.

Legal briefs are necessarily filled with abstract concepts that are difficult to explain. Nothing clarifies their meaning as well as examples. One can describe the interpretive canon *noscitur a sociis* as the concept that a word is given meaning by the words with which it is associated. But the reader probably won't really grasp what you're talking about until you give an example similar to the one we gave earlier: "pins, staples, rivets, nails, and spikes." In that context, "pins" couldn't refer to lapel ornaments, "staples" couldn't refer to standard foodstuffs, "nails" couldn't refer to fingernails, and "spikes" couldn't refer to hairstyles.

43. Make it interesting.

To say that your writing must be clear and brief is not to say that it must be dull. Of course, you should employ the usual devices of effective writing: simile, metaphor, understatement, analogy, and antithesis. But you shouldn't use these or other devices of style for their own sake. They are helpful

> "[I]n everything monotony is the mother of boredom."
> —Cicero

only if they cause the serious legal points you're making to be more vivid, more lively, and hence more memorable.

Three simple ways to add interest to your writing are to enliven your word choices, to mix up your sentence structures, and to vary your sentence lengths. With words, ask yourself whether there's a more colorful way to put it. With sentences, guard against falling into a monotonous subject–verb–object rut—especially when it's the same subject, sentence after sentence. And remember that an occasional arrestingly short sentence can deliver real punch ("This wolf comes as a wolf").

44. Banish jargon, hackneyed expressions, and needless Latin.

By "jargon" we mean the words and phrases used almost exclusively by lawyers in place of plain-English words and phrases that express the same thought. Jargon adds nothing but a phony air of expertise. A *nexus*, for example, is nothing more or less than a link or a connection. And what is *the instant case?* Does it have anything to do with instant coffee? Alas, to tell the truth, it's no different from *this case* or even *here*. Write normal English. *Such* as a demonstrative adjective (*such action*) can almost always be replaced with the good old normal English *this* or *that*. And *hereinbefore* with *earlier*. And *pursuant to* with *under*. The key is to avoid words that would cause people to look at you funny if you used them at a party. Pretend that you're telling your story to some friends in your living room; that's how you should tell it to the court.

Give the reader credit for having a brain—and show that you have one, too. Don't leave your common sense at the door. If your brief repeatedly refers to the Secretary of Transportation and mentions no other Secretary, it is silly to specify parenthetically, the first time you mention the Secretary of Transportation, "(hereinafter 'the Secretary')." No one will think that your later references to "the Secretary" denote the Secretary of Defense, or perhaps your own secretary.

Hackneyed expressions are verbal formulations that were wonderfully vivid when first used, but whose vividness, through overuse, no longer pleases but bores. Such-and-such a case "and its progeny" is a good example. Or the assertion that an argument is "fatally flawed" or "flies in the face of" something; that your adversary is "painting with a broad brush"; that a claim isn't "viable"; that the "parameters" of a rule aren't settled; or that something is true "beyond peradventure of doubt."

> "The readability of Holmes and Cardozo is due in part to their mastery of the native tongue and subjugation of the acquired language of the law."
>
> —Hon. Wiley B. Rutledge

The test is: have you seen the vivid phrase a lot? If so, odds are it's a cliché.

Some Latin expressions are convenient shorthand for rules or principles that have no English shorthand equivalent (*res ipsa loquitur*, for example, or *inclusio unius est exclusio alterius*). But avoid using other Latin phrases, such as *ceteris paribus*, *inter alia*, *mutatis mutandis*, and *pari passu*. Judges are permitted to show off in this fashion, but lawyers must not. And the judge who does not happen to know the obscure Latin phrase you have flaunted will think you a twit.

45. Consider using contractions occasionally—or not.

The Garner view: In a book I wrote in 1991, this advice appeared: "Contractions are usually out of place in legal writing. Instead of *can't*, prefer *cannot*; instead of *won't*, *will not*; and so forth. . . . Common contractions such as *hasn't* and *didn't* may be perfectly appropriate in correspondence, but not in court papers."[38] Eleven years later, in the second

---

38 Garner, *The Elements of Legal Style* 81 (1991).

edition, the relevant passage was dramatically changed: "You might well have heard that contractions don't belong in legal writing. The view seems to be that they aren't professional. But that's just a shibboleth. In fact, the decision whether to use a contraction often boils down to this: do I want to sound natural, or do I want to sound stuffy?"[39]

What accounted for the about-face? Mostly the influence of John R. Trimble, author of a classic book on writing,[40] who urged a change of position on grounds that contractions help you achieve a more conversational rhythm in your writing. He's not the only respected expert advocating contractions.[41] Unsurprisingly, empirical studies have shown that frequent contractions enhance readability.[42] And then, of course, there are the respected legal writers who've used contractions as a way of making their writing more readable, such as Clarence Darrow, Griffin B. Bell, Richard A. Posner, Frank Easterbrook, and Alex Kozinski. And consider that every President since President Ford in 1975 has

---

39 Garner, *The Elements of Legal Style* 81 (2d ed. 2000).

40 John R. Trimble, *Writing with Style: Conversations on the Art of Writing* (2d ed. 2000).

41 *See* William Zinsser, *On Writing Well* 75 (6th ed. 1998) ("Your style will be warmer and truer to your own personality if you use contractions like *won't* and *can't* when they fit comfortably into what you're writing."); David W. Ewing, *Writing for Results in Business, Government, and the Professions* 358 (1974) ("Such common contractions as *it's*, *that's*, *they're*, and *she'll* are correct in almost all written communications in business and the professions."); Rudolf Flesch, *The Art of Readable Writing* 82 (1949) ("[t]he most conspicuous and handiest device of [writing readably] is to use contractions.").

42 Wayne A. Danielson & Dominic I. Lasorsa, *A New Readability Formula Based on the Stylistic Age of Novels*, 33 J. Reading 194, 196 (1989).

used contractions in the State of the Union Address. Did these contractions diminish the perceived "dignity" of the addresses? Seemingly not.

Contractions ought to become more widespread in legal writing. That includes briefs and judicial opinions. But they shouldn't appear at every single turn—only when, in speaking, one would most naturally use a contraction.

As for the idea that contractions may arouse negativity in the judicial mind, it doesn't square with experience. If contractions are distractingly beneath the judicial reader's dignity, then what kind of reaction occurs when judges' eyes are accosted with contractions on virtually every page of the *New Yorker*, *Time*, *Newsweek*, and the *Economist?* In some sentences, are not contractions all but obligatory? Do you not think?

(Aside: In his ensuing discussion of contractions, Justice Scalia disparages my insistence that we make this text gender-neutral. He yielded on the point in part, I think, because my usage books recommend this strategy in extended entries entitled "Sexism," and I'm grateful that he did so. In my view, that's an instance of adopting a convention to avoid distracting readers. So I advocate "invisible gender-neutrality."[43] In a way it's similar to the debate on contractions: I think the uncontracted words will distract or subliminally repel readers, and he thinks the contraction

---

43 *See* Garner, "Bias-Free Language," in *The Chicago Manual of Style* § 5.204, at 233 (15th ed. 2003).

will distract or subliminally repel readers. It's an empirical issue that will no doubt be tested in years to come.)

The Scalia view: Clarence Darrow and Griffin Bell may well have made their "legal writings" more readable by occasional use of contractions. But I doubt that the legal writings thus vulgarized (look the word up before you consider it too strong) included their briefs filed in court. As for Judges Posner, Easterbrook, and Kozinski, life tenure is a wonderful thing; neither they nor any client of theirs pays a price for their contractions. (Kozinski, for Pete's sake, has been known to write an opinion with 200 movie titles embedded within it.) And the State of the Union Address is not writing but (hello!) an address. The rules for oral communication are different. A proper test would be whether Presidents use contractions in their signing statements, veto messages, and executive orders. (They do not.)

The issue before us here, however, in this advice-giving treatise on legal argumentation, is quite simply whether contractions are (1) *more* or (2) *less* likely to advance your cause. I have no doubt that (2) is the answer. All of us employ different styles of speech, and of writing, for different occasions. Some words perfectly proper in some circumstances are jarringly inapt in others. That is why good dictionaries have the designation "*colloq.*" Written forensic presentations have always been thought demanding of more formal expression, just as oral forensic presentations are demanding (see § 73) of more formal attire.

Formality bespeaks dignity. I guarantee that if you use contractions in your written submissions, some judges—including many who are not offended by the use of contractions in the *New Yorker*, *Time*, *Vogue*, the *Rolling Stone*, *Field and Stream*, and other publications not addressed to black-robed judges engaged in the exercise of their august governmental powers—will take it as an affront to the dignity of the court. ("Why next, to ensure a more 'conversational' environment, this cheeky fellow will have us shed our robes, and start calling us by our first names!") And those judges who don't take offense will not understand your brief, or vote for your case, one whit more readily. There is, in short, something to be lost, and nothing whatever to be gained. Unless, of course, you and your client share with my esteemed coauthor the Jacobin passion to bring written discourse in the forum down to the level of spoken discourse in the marketplace.

As for the telling example "Do you not think?": that sounds klutzy for two reasons. First, because it is colloquial in dropping the last word, "so," and the combination of informality and formality is absurd. And second, because it is almost impossible to conjure up an example of formal writing that asks the reader a direct question; the very act of asking is *inherently* informal, so couching the question in formal terms seems absurd. (Yes, formal writings sometimes contain rhetorical questions that answer themselves; they are not seeking the reader's opinion, but are addressed, so to speak, to the Spirit of Reason.) Moreover, surely writings that use contractions also confront clumsy patches that must be written around—unless my coauthor employs the unacceptable "ain't" or suddenly inserts among his folksy contractions the very formal "am I not."

Which suggests another comment that is almost a point of personal privilege: I find it incomprehensible that my esteemed coauthor, who has displayed the inventiveness of a DaVinci and the imagination of a Tolkien in devising circumlocutions that have purged from my contributions to this volume (at some stylistic cost) all use of "he" as the traditional, generic, unisex reference to a human being—incomprehensible, I say, that this same coauthor should speak disparagingly of "shibboleths," and feign inability to come up with an acceptable substitute for the clumsy "Do you not think?" (Try "Is that not so?" or "Would you not agree?")

(Response to aside: Invisible, my eye. I'll bet you can spot the places where force or simplicity has been sacrificed to second-best circumlocution. As for distraction: To those of us who believe that "he" means, and has always meant, "he or she" when not referring to a male antecedent, the ritual shunning of it to avoid giving offense to gender-neutralizers is . . . well, distracting.)

46. Avoid acronyms. Use the parties' names.

Acronyms are mainly for the convenience of the writer or speaker. Don't burden your reader or listener with many of them, especially unfamiliar ones. FBI and IRS are OK, but not CPSC and FHLBB. You may be surprised how easy it is to avoid a brief of alphabet soup—and from the reader's point of

> "One day we may all be buried under an avalanche of acronyms."
> —John Algeo

view (which is the only point of view that counts) it is worth the effort. If the Consumer Product Safety Commission plays a prominent role in your case, and no other agency has any part at all, call it "the Commission," or even simply "the agency." If the case concerns the Prosecutorial Remedies and Other Tools to end the Exploitation of Children Today Act of 2003 (117 Stat. 650), foil the drafters by refusing to call it "the PROTECT Act"; just "the Act" will do.

The reason for avoiding acronyms is well exemplified in a fictional passage devised by Judge Daniel Friedman:

> [I]t is not unusual to read a sentence such as this in a brief: "The Port Association of Freight Forwarders (PAFF) entered into an Agreement Covering Loading Practices in the Inner Harbor (ACLPIH) with the Seattle Chapter of the Union of Warehousemen and Stevedores (SCUWS)." Two pages later, the following appears: "Under the ACLPIH, SCUWS was required to consult with PAFF before taking that action." This problem could be avoided if, instead of using these initials, the writer employed shorthand terms, such as "Association," "Agreement," and "Union." In place of the gibberish just quoted, the sentence would be fully comprehensible and succinct: "Under the Agreement, the

Union was required to consult with the Association before taking that action."[44]

Refer to the parties by their names rather than their status in the litigation (plaintiff, respondent, etc.). There are good reasons for this. Sometimes, in reading briefs, judges will get confused about who is on the up-side and who on the down-side—and will have to flip back to the cover to see who "Petitioner" is. Moreover, the petitioner here may have been the defendant at trial, and the respondent on the first appeal. This can make the record on appeal confusing if status-names are used in the briefing and argument at each level. Everett Jones, however, is always and everywhere, at all stages of the litigation, Jones.

Some mistakenly advise that you should try to personalize your client and depersonalize the opposing party by calling the former "Jones" and the latter "Defendant." This is much too cute; rather than depersonalizing the defendant, it will annoy the court and ruin the story.

Sometimes each side of the case has multiple parties, so it is impossible to use a single name. No problem. If they are all railroads, refer to them as "the railroads"; or if all debtors, call them "the debtors." If they are a mishmash, pick the name of one of them and define that to include the entire group. For example, "The petitioners (collectively, 'Exxon') claimed below that . . . ."

---

44 Hon. Daniel M. Friedman, "Winning on Appeal," in *Appellate Practice Manual* 129, 134 (Priscilla Anne Schwab ed., 1992).

Here, as everywhere, clarity governs all. It sometimes makes sense to use terms like "general contractor," "owner," and "subcontractor" if that will identify the cast of characters in a way that makes the story more comprehensible.

47. Don't overuse italics; don't use bold type except in headings; don't use underlining at all.

Italicize to emphasize, but do it sparingly. Remember that when too much is emphasized, nothing is. Constant italicizing gives your brief the tone of an adolescent diary, which is not what you should be striving for.

Whenever possible, replace your italics with the device that provides the usual means of emphasis in written English: word order. In phrasing sentences, try to put the punch word at the end. Instead of writing "She held *a knife* in her hand," write "What she held in her hand was a knife." The latter formulation gives equivalent prominence to the desired word but sounds less excited. But when the only means of making your thought clear is to italicize a word or phrase, do it.

Some brief-writers ill-advisedly use boldface type within normal text. The result is visually repulsive. Reserve boldface for headings.

As for underlining, it's a crude throwback: that's what writers used in typewriting—when italics weren't possible. Nobody using a computer in the 21st century should be underlining text. To the extent that *The Bluebook* suggests otherwise, it should be revised.

48. Describe and cite authorities with scrupulous accuracy.

Persuasive briefing induces the court to draw favorable conclusions from accurate descriptions of your authorities. It never distorts cases to fit the facts. The impression you want to make on the court—that you're knowledgeable and even expert—will be compromised by any misdescription that opposing counsel brings to the court's attention. If a case is only close but not completely in point, say so. Then explain why the difference is insubstantial and should not affect the outcome.

Make faithful and accurate use of the conventional introductory signals, as set forth in *The Bluebook*[45] or the *ALWD Citation Manual*[46]—one of which should always be on your desk. If another style manual is required in your state courts, use it. When you cite a case with no introductory signal, you're affirming to the court that this case explicitly *holds* what you have just said. If it is an alternative holding, say so with the parenthetical "(alternative holding)." If the proposition you have propounded is not stated in the case but necessarily follows from its holding, introduce the case by *See*. When the case you cite is merely analogous authority for the proposition you have stated, introduce it with the signal *Cf*. Show a contrary holding with *Contra*, and a case

---

45 *The Bluebook: A Uniform System of Citation* § 1.2, at 46–48 (18th ed. 2005).

46 *ALWD Citation Manual: A Professional System of Citation* § 44.3, at 324–25 (3d ed. 2006).

from whose reasoning a contrary holding necessarily follows with *But see.* And so forth. Consult your citation guide.

When even one of your citations fails to live up to your introductory signal, or is not parenthetically qualified when necessary, all the rest of your citations inevitably become suspect. Remember the evidentiary maxim, which pretty well describes the way people (including judges) generally react to intentional or even careless distortion: *falsus in uno, falsus in omnibus.* False in one respect, false in all.

And put your citations in the form most convenient for the generalist judge. In referring to a governing text, cite the official code. Some briefs cite sections of the original enactment as contained in session laws (in the federal system, "Stat." cites) rather than the sections as codified (e.g., the United States Code). For example, a brief may refer to "section 502(a)(3) of ERISA" to identify a provision of the Employee Retirement Income Security Act of 1974, Pub. L. No. 93-406, Tit. I, 88 Stat. 829, even though that provision is now codified at 29 U.S.C. § 1132(a)(3). It's easy to understand why this practice arises, since before codification the *only* source for citation is the session law; all the early law-review articles and commentaries refer to "section __ of the Act," and practitioners specializing in that field become accustomed to using that form of reference. But once codification has occurred, this practice can do nothing but confuse. Since proper citation form requires the Code section, we end up with a brief that refers to § 502(a)(3), followed (at least the first time that designation is used) by a citation of § 1132(a)(3). Worse, sometimes a brief that does this then adds an appendix using only the Code sections, leaving it to the reader to figure out which one is § 502. Once an act has been codified, refer to the Code sections; to do otherwise is to frustrate the whole purpose of codification. The judges may not be as familiar with the original act as you are, and they are accustomed to working from the Code. Make their job easier by using Code references consistently.

Professionalism is largely a matter of thwarting Murphy's Law: if something can go wrong, it will. Anyone who has ever written a book or article knows that errors can creep in with alarming ease. So you create safeguards that prevent things from going awry. Verify your quotations and citations as you enter them into a draft. Ensure that someone other than the researcher verifies them a second time. Ensure that others read the brief—not just those who collaborated in producing it. You yourself proofread it two more times than you think necessary. And KeyCite or Shepardize the citations once again before filing the brief—perhaps while creating the Table of Authorities.

49. Cite authorities sparingly.

You're not writing a treatise, a law-review article, or a comprehensive *Corpus Juris* annotation. You are trying to persuade one court in one jurisdiction. And what you're trying to persuade it of is not your (or your junior associate's) skill and tenacity at legal research. You will win no points, therefore, for digging out and including in your brief every relevant case. On the contrary, the glut of authority will only be distracting. What counts is not how many authorities you cite, but how well you use them.

> "[T]he fact is that in his brief, the lawyer seems oppressed with the feeling that his reasoning must be the servant of his authorities, with the result that his argument often becomes heavy from forced subordination, when it might be lightened by using the cases merely to illustrate, like pictures in a book."
> —Howard C. Westwood

As for governing authority, if the point you are making is relevant to your reasoning but is neither controversial nor likely to be controverted, a single citation (the more recent the better) will suffice. Anything more is just showing off to an unappreciative audience. But if the point is central to your case and likely to be contested, not only cite the case but concisely describe its facts and its holding. And follow that description by citing other governing cases (*Accord Smith v. Jones, Roe v. Doe*).

If there is no governing authority in point, your resort to persuasive authority may require more extensive citation to show that the rule you are urging has been accepted in other jurisdictions. (For example: "Every other jurisdiction that has confronted this question has reached the same conclusion. *See Smith v. Jones*, 972 P.2d 1294 (Cal. 1998); *Roe v. Doe*, 649 N.E.2d 1391 (N.Y. 1995); *Riley v. Silberman*, 593 S.E.2d 930 (Va. 2003).") If persuasive authority is overwhelmingly in your favor but not uniformly so, you may have to resort to a footnote showing all the courts in your favor, followed by a *But see* citation of the few courts that are opposed. And citing an ALR annotation on point will be helpful.

Secondary authorities (treatises, law-review articles, case annotations) help confirm your analysis of trends in the law, general background (supporting, for example, your statement that before the statute at issue was adopted, the law was thus-and-so), and your view about what is the "best" rule with the most desirable policy consequences. It's superfluous—and hence harmful—to cite a secondary authority for a proposition clearly established by governing authority.

Don't expect the court, or even the law clerks, to read your secondary authority; they will at most check to see that it supports the point you make. They will therefore be persuaded not by the *reasoning* of your secondary authority but only by the *fact* that its author agrees with you. And the force of the persuasion will vary directly with the prominence of the author. Thus, except as a convenient way to refer the court to a compendium of cases, it's not much help to bring to the court's attention the fact that a student law-review note is on your side. Use it only when you have nothing else.

50. Quote authorities more sparingly still.

We've said that it pays to quote directly from a case setting forth your major premise. But it doesn't pay to string along quotation after quotation for the rest of the paragraph. A remarkably large number of lawyers seem to believe that their briefs are improved if each thought is expressed in the words of a governing case. The contrary is true. After you have established your major premise, it will be your reasoning that interests the court, and this is almost always more clearly and forcefully expressed in your own words than in the stringing together of quotations from various cases. Such a cut-and-paste approach also produces an air of artificiality, even of lack of self-assurance. You want the court to develop confidence in your reasoning—not in your ability to gopher up supporting quotations. Say what you know to be the law, and support it by citing a case that holds precisely that.

> "Quotations from cases are effective only if used sparingly. Quoting at length from opinion after opinion is a lazy way of writing a brief, and the finished product is likely to be unconvincing. Long before the brief approaches its end, the reader has begun to skip over the quotations."
> —Hon. Daniel M. Friedman

Be especially loath to use a lengthy, indented quotation. It invites skipping. In fact, many block quotes have probably never been read by anyone. So never let your point be made only in the indented quotation. State the point, and then support it with the quotation ("As Chief Justice Marshall expressed it: . . ."). This is, to be sure, iteration (yet another reason to avoid block quotes). But iteration that simultaneously buttresses with authority is sometimes effective.

If you can't weave quotations deftly into the fabric of your prose—especially the block quotations—abjure them altogether and paraphrase instead. If you ever use a series of quotations, remember that you must supply connective tissue between them—words to take the reader smoothly from one quotation to the next. Back-to-back quotations with no connectives are verboten.

51. Swear off substantive footnotes—or not.

The Garner view: Put no substantive point in a footnote—none, at least, that you consider important to your argument. There are several reasons for this, but the best is that many judges don't read footnotes. Some courts have even announced that they won't consider any argument raised exclusively in a footnote.[47] Ah, yes, you are accustomed to seeing lengthy footnotes in judicial opinions and in law-review articles. But the authors of judicial opinions don't

---

47 *E.g., NSTAR Elec. & Gas Corp. v. FERC,* 481 F.3d 794, 799–800 (D.C. Cir. 2007) ("[T]his argument is found in a single footnote in NSTAR's opening brief, and such a reference is not enough to raise an issue for our review."); *Smithkline Beecham Corp. v. Apotex Corp.,* 439 F.3d 1312, 1320 (Fed. Cir. 2006) ("[A]rguments raised in footnotes are not preserved."); *Lutwin v. Thompson,* 361 F.3d 146, 148 n.1 (2d Cir. 2004) ("We decline to consider this argument because '[a] contention is not sufficiently presented for appeal if it is conclusorily asserted only in a footnote.'" [quoting *Tolbert v. Queens College,* 242 F.3d 58, 75 (2d Cir. 2001)]); *U.S. v. Dairy Farmers of Am., Inc.,* 426 F.3d 850, 856 (6th Cir. 2005) ("An argument contained only in a footnote does not preserve an issue for our review."); *Sledd v. Lindsay,* 102 F.3d 282, 288 (7th Cir. 1996); *Equipment Mfrs. Inst. v. Janklow,* 300 F.3d 842, 848 n.2 (8th Cir. 2002) ("[T]his Court will not consider a claim improperly presented in a footnote."); *Bakalis v. Golembeski,* 35 F.3d 318, 326 n.8 (7th Cir. 1994) (An argument "made only in a footnote in the opening brief" and "not fully developed until the reply brief . . . is deemed waived."); *People v. Crosswhite,* 124 Cal. Rptr. 2d 301, 306 n.5 (Ct. App. 2001) ("This argument is waived by raising it only in a footnote under an argument heading which gives no notice of the contention."); *Roberts v. Worcester Redev. Auth.,* 759 N.E.2d 1220, 1227 n.11 (Mass. App. Ct. 2001) ("We are not required to address an argument raised in a footnote.").

win or lose by keeping their audience's attention. And law-review writers are generally most interested in demonstrating their scholarship. Whatever the value of substantive footnotes in those contexts—and many think they ought to be seriously curbed there as well—they have no place in a brief. If the point is not important enough to be in the text, it's not important enough to be in the brief.

You may recoil from the blackletter admonition here. But a year or two after deciding that you'll never put a sentence in a footnote (reference notes containing only bibliographical material are okay), you'll probably be surprised at how easy that resolution is to keep.

A Scalia qualification: In my view, the preceding advice is too categorical. The Solicitor General of the United States, after all, is a highly skilled and experienced advocate, and the briefs of that office almost always contain substantive footnotes.

It is assuredly true that nothing really important to the decision should be in a footnote. And it's even true that, in most courts before which you are likely to appear, nothing of substance should be in a footnote. But in those courts with a relatively limited docket, accustomed to issuing detailed and exhaustive opinions, some relatively unimportant matters are worth discussing below the text. As Chief Judge Frank Easterbrook of the Seventh Circuit, himself a former Deputy Solicitor General, has told us in a letter:

> The SG's style, at least when I was there, was to write two briefs: one for all the Justices as they prepared for oral

argument, and another for the Justice assigned to write the opinion. The straightforward, punchy argument appeared in the text of the brief. The extra details were in the footnotes. The office also used footnotes to anticipate the other side's weaker arguments and to address arguments that the other side never made—but that the Justices or their clerks might think up.

It is bad to waste space in the text of a brief addressing arguments never made, but it is worse to know that a bright person might come up with an argument, have a ready answer, omit it from the brief, and then find from the opinion that the judge has thought up the argument *but not the answer.* Putting such information in footnotes makes it possible to file a cogent and streamlined brief, the sort of thing that will persuade on first reading, while keeping potentially helpful elaboration available for the judge to consult later.

I know of no court that will categorically not consider substantive footnotes. The citations contained in my coauthor's scary footnote pertain to the raising of fundamentally new claims or new arguments—for example, making a Due Process Clause argument in a footnote when all the rest of the brief relies on the Sixth Amendment. That shouldn't be done anyway. But providing useful (though less than essential) support for an argument made in text is quite different. And more different still is a footnoted response to a weak argument made by the other side. These footnotes may not be read; but if read they will be considered.

52. Consider putting citations in footnotes—or not.

The Garner view: I've made it something of a cause célèbre to reform the way citations are interlarded in lawyers' texts.[48] Since 1992, I've recommended putting all bibliographic material (volume numbers and page numbers) in footnotes but avoiding putting any substantive text (complete sentences) there. Nothing should appear in a footnote that anyone should have to read—only what someone might consult for looking up a reference.[49] Under this system of subordinating citations, readers should never be asked to look down at footnotes—there's nothing significant there because the important authorities have been named and discussed in the text ("Three years ago in *Flom v. Baumgartner,* this Court held that . . .").

Using this system, while describing in the text the major authorities you're relying on, has several advantages: (1) visually, the important material on the page, the discussion of authorities through close reasoning, is most prominent instead of the least important information, namely, the volume and page numbers; (2) disjointed thoughts, which are rampant in briefs, are immediately exposed for what they are; (3) poor paragraphing gets exposed; (4) discussion of governing and persuasive authorities is enhanced because it can no longer be buried in parentheticals following citations; and (5) the prose more closely follows

---

48 *See* William Glaberson, *Legal Citations on Trial in Innovation v. Tradition,* N.Y. Times, 8 July 2001, at 1, 16.

49 *See Garner on Language and Writing* 436–55, 460–71 (2008).

the practices of the most accomplished nonfiction writers of our day. Although this technique improves the prose, it concededly makes greater demands on the writer, who must maintain a tighter train of thought. Readers need no longer skip over long swaths of bibliographic characters in the middle of the page (a holdover of typewriting style). Meanwhile, those readers who are critically evaluating your cited authorities—your adversaries and judges—can still see what you've cited.

Whether this system will gain widespread acceptance within the profession remains to be seen. Many judges and lawyers have adopted it,[50] and their numbers are increasing. We should measure progress in decades. It is with no small degree of sadness that I note my inability to persuade my coauthor to use this method for the improvement of judicial writing generally. One of his favorite sayings is that "whatever doesn't help hurts," and it's inconceivable that 535 U.S. 274, 276, 122 S.Ct. 1414, 1416, 152 L.Ed.2d 437, 439 helps anyone who's trying to get through a paragraph. Meanwhile, his worries about "crabby judges" have rarely if ever been borne out among the many hundreds of lawyers who years ago adopted my recommendation and continue to follow it. Quite the opposite: they report that they routinely meet with positive outcomes—in part because they write more compellingly as a result of this technique.

The Scalia view: Alas, I disapprove this novel suggestion. You cannot make your product more readable to the careful

---

50 For cited examples, see Garner. *Legal Writing in Plain English* (2001).

lawyer by putting the entire citation material (case name, court, date, volume, and page) in a footnote—because the careful lawyer wants to know, while reading along, what the authority is for what you say. So, far from enabling the reader's eyes to run smoothly across a text uninterrupted by this ugly material, you would force the eyes to bounce repeatedly from text to footnote.

My coauthor's solution to this problem is to "weave" the name of the court and the case name (and the date?) into the text ("As the Supreme Court of the United States said in the 1959 case of *Schwarz v. Schwarz*,[1] . . ."). I doubt that this can be done (without sounding silly) for all the citations that a brief contains. But if it can, it will surely place undue emphasis upon, and inflate the text with, details inessential to the reasoning. I will rarely want the court, name, and date of a case thrust in my face, so to speak, by inclusion in the narrative text as though it's really important. Ordinarily, such information can better be conveyed, almost subliminally, in a running citation. Lawyers are used to skipping over these signals quickly and moving on to the next sentence. If in this respect legal-writing style differs from other writing style, it is only because lawyers must evaluate statements not on the basis of whether they make sense but on the basis of whether some governing authority said so.

Of course, whatever the merits of this debate, the conclusive reason not to accept Garner's novel suggestion is that it is novel. Judges are uncomfortable with change, and it is a sure thing that some crabby judges will dislike this one. You should no more try to convert the court to citation-free text at your client's expense than you should try to convert it to colorful ties or casual-Friday attire at oral argument. Now if Garner wanted to make a really useful suggestion, he might suggest avoiding, wherever possible, the insertion of lengthy citations in the middle of a sentence. That is easy to achieve, and certain not to offend.

53. Make the relevant text readily available to the court.

A text worth discussing is a text worth reading. Make sure that the *entirety* of the text you are relying on (or that your adversary is mistakenly relying on) appears somewhere in your brief. This is an exception to our caution against block quotations. If the statutory or other material is lengthy, put it in an appendix to the brief. (Placing some or most of it in a Joint Appendix is not enough; judges are distracted and annoyed by having to flip back and forth between volumes for material that is central to the case.) By the *entirety* of the text we mean not only the dispositive provision but also other portions that you claim bear on interpretation of the dispositive provision. Whatever text forms part of your argument should be not merely cited but reproduced in your brief.

And reproduce the text of the statute, ordinance, or regulation as it existed at the relevant time. If it has been amended since, that should be indicated in a citation. Sometimes earlier or later versions of the text are relevant to its interpretation. When that is so, reproduce the other versions—with the differences shown in italics or redlining.

54. Don't spoil your product with poor typography.

When business consultants make a presentation to a prospective client, they come forward with a professionally produced, bound proposal. They understand that to get business they must persuade, and that good visuals help. The same is true for persuading judges. A brief that is in an ugly typeface, with crowded lines, will not invite careful perusal. In the days when briefs had to be printed, counsel (and the court) could rely on a knowledgeable printer to produce a readily legible product. Now that lawyers can produce their own briefs using desktop-publishing software, the filed product is often disastrous.

> "I have seen firms spend hundreds of thousands of dollars on technology only to make their briefs and other documents look like they were typed on a 1940 Underwood. Never use Courier."
>
> —Mark P. Painter

The Supreme Court of the United States has set forth printing requirements in its rule 33. If the court in which you're filing has no such requirements, or significantly less rigorous ones, you should consider using the Supreme Court rules as a model. Better still, the United States Court of Appeals for the Seventh Circuit has posted on its website detailed, sage guidance for proper printing.

If necessary, hire someone to do the job right.

136

Oral
Argument

Introduction

55. Appreciate the importance of oral argument, and know your objectives.

Many lawyers view oral argument as just a formality, especially in courts that make a practice of reading the briefs in advance. Sure, it gives counsel a chance to show off before the client. But as far as affecting the outcome is concerned, what can 20 minutes or half an hour of oral argument add to what the judge has already learned from reading a few hundred pages of briefs, underlining significant passages and annotating the margins?

This skepticism has proved false in every study of judicial behavior we know. Does oral argument change a well-prepared judge's mind? Rarely. What often happens, though, is that the judge is undecided at the time of oral argument (the case is a close one), and oral argument makes the difference. It makes the difference because it provides information and perspective that the briefs don't and can't contain.

A brief is logical and sequential. If it contains five points, they will often be addressed in some logical order, not necessarily in the order of their importance. The amount of space devoted to each point, moreover, has more to do with its complexity than its strength. Someone who has read your brief, therefore—and especially someone who has read it some days ago—may have a distorted impression of your case. The reader may think that point #1, which it takes a third of your brief to explain, is the most significant aspect of your argument, whereas in fact point #3, which covers half as many pages, is really your trump card. Oral argument can put things in perspective: "Your Honors, we have four points to our brief, all of which we think merit your attention. But the heart of our argument is point #3, on issue preclusion, and I'll turn to that now."

Oral argument also provides information that the brief can't contain. Most obviously, it gives the appellee an opportunity to reply to responses and new points contained in the appellant's reply brief. At least as important, it provides both sides the opportunity to answer questions that have arisen in the judges' minds. The most obvious of these should have been anticipated and answered in the briefing, but repetition of the answer to a persistent doubter can be helpful. And the judges are bound to have in mind questions unanticipated by the briefs—either because the answer is too obvious or because the question is too subtle. Oral argument is the time to lay these judicial doubts to rest. And finally, the quality of oral argument can convey to the court that the brief already submitted is the product of a highly capable and trustworthy attorney, intimately familiar with the facts and the law of the case.

In descending order of importance, your objectives in oral argument are these:

1. To answer any questions and satisfy any doubts that have arisen in the judges' minds.

2. If you're counsel for the appellee, to answer new and telling points raised in the appellant's reply brief. Oral argument is your only chance.

3. To call to the judges' minds and reinforce the substantive points made in your brief.

4. To demonstrate to the court, by the substance and manner of your presentation, that you are trustworthy, open, and forthright.

5. To demonstrate to the court, by the substance and manner of your presentation, that you have thought long and hard about this case and are familiar with all its details.

6. To demonstrate to the court, mostly by the manner of your presentation, that you are likable and not meanspirited.

Long-Term Preparation

56. Prepare yourself generally as a public speaker.

Everybody has a personal manner of speaking, and it's a mistake to try to be what you're not. So don't try to emulate Perry Mason. Be yourself. But avoid the common mistakes in delivery that advocates make. You'll find that avoiding some of them takes practice.

Don't speak fast. Machine-gun presentations, even when perfectly well understood, are ineffective. Most people can process information only at a moderate rate. When ideas—even the best ideas—come tumbling forth too fast, they're apt to induce either headache or inattention. (There is probably such a thing as speaking too slowly, but few have ever observed it.) Working on a slower presentation is likely to be difficult but worth the trouble.

> "Many speakers soon after starting reach a monotone pitched about three notes above the ordinary talking key and hold the pitch without variation until the end of their address. This has the most soporific effect upon the court and the jury and makes them wish for a bed where they might attain to a state of unconsciousness."
> —Henry S. Wilcox

Adjust the volume of your voice to the surroundings and the sound-enhancement equipment available. The decibel level of your delivery should be conversational, not oratorical, throughout. The judges should be able to hear you with ease and without discomfort. If you're speaking so softly that they miss snippets of your presentation, or so loudly that listening is painful, they'll rarely ask you to adjust your volume; but they'll often tune you out. Crescendos and fortissimos of delivery may be effective in a declamatory oration, when appeal to emotion and incitement to action are the object. They're decidedly ineffective in the courtroom, where counsel's implicit message to the court is "Let us reason together."

Lower the pitch of your voice. A high and shrill tone does not inspire confidence. You must speak, of course, with the voice you've been given, but voices can be improved over time. Expand your lower register through practice. This doesn't mean that you should sound like a radio announcer. But realize that your natural tone tends to be elevated by excitement, or by the desire to drive home a point.

Speak distinctly. Oral argument is not the place to drop consonants and slur your words. Practice enunciating each word clearly and separating it from the words before and after. Most judges, if they have not understood a phrase or sentence of your presentation, will not ask you to repeat it—and your point will have been lost.

Purge your speech of "ums" and "ers." Such "filler" sounds do nothing but distract. Far better, if necessary, simply to pause between words. But avoiding "ums" and "ers" can't be achieved by practicing it the night before argument. Like clear enunciation and modulation of volume and pitch, it's something you must put into practice in your daily speech if you aspire to be an oral advocate. One way to sensitize yourself to "ums" and "ers" is to tape-record or videotape a practice presentation. That exercise in self-observation can be uncomfortable, but it can induce dramatic improvement.

57. Master the preferred pronunciations of English words, legal terms, and proper names.

Like Eliza Doolittle in *My Fair Lady*, you'll be thought either sophisticated or simple-minded, knowledgeable or ignorant, not just by what you say but also by how you say it. Besides avoiding dialect (*ain't*), informalisms (*yeah*), and common illiteracies (misusing *infer* for *imply*, saying "*nuculus*" for *nucleus*, or pronouncing *athlete* and *realtor* as though they were three-syllable words), ensure that your pronunciation of proper names, legal terminology, and even everyday English words is orthodox. The lawyer who refers to Chief Justice Taney as /**tay**-nee/ instead of the correct /**taw**-nee/, who mentions the rule of lenity as if it were /**leen**-i-tee/, or who invokes the maxim /no-site-tur eh soh-keys/ (*noscitur a sociis* is pronounced /**nos**-i-ter ay [*or* ah] **soh**-shee-is/) will never be mistaken for an expert.

So how does one learn "preferred" pronunciations? And by whom are they preferred? Fair questions both.

Many words have more than one pronunciation. Sometimes the variants are equally acceptable (for example, *aunt* can be either /ant/ or /ahnt/). But more often (in *often*, the *-t-* is preferably silent) one pronunciation typifies educated speech and the other uneducated speech. Naturally, being a professional with an advanced degree—unless your persona is that of a folksy, down-home lawyer—you'll do

144

better to stay within the mainstream of standard pronunciation. Hence "preferred" means "preferred by well-educated people."

When in doubt, consult a good, current desktop dictionary. Better yet, consult a resource such as Charles Harrington Elster's *Big Book of Beastly Mispronunciations* (2d ed. 2006). There you'll find excellent, engaging essays on the best ways to say all the most troublesome words in the language. Be prepared to learn that you've been mispronouncing *comptroller, coupon, err, flaccid, heinous,* and *schism* all these years. Elster has been the pronunciation editor of *Black's Law Dictionary* since the seventh edition of 1999, so you can find authoritative, easy-to-follow pronunciations of distinctively legal terms in the current editions of that work.

> "Of pronunciations, the incorrect are the result either of illiterate association or of imperfect education. In conversation these may turn the finest of reasoning into ridicule, which may deprive the speaker of the respect and attention of his audience."
> —Frank H. Vizetelly

Pronunciation can be a tricky matter. For one thing, there are regional variations. *Voir dire* is pronounced /vwahr **deer**/ almost universally, but it's /vohr **dyer**/ in Texas and surrounding states. A Texas lawyer would be foolish to appear in a Texas courtroom and pronounce the phrase like some newly arrived outlander. And what's a visiting lawyer who's been admitted in Texas *pro hac vice* (/proh hahk **vee**-chay/ or /proh hak **veye**-see/) to do? Probably the best course, if you're linguistically flexible enough, is to use the local pronunciation in that proceeding, offensive as it may be to your ear. Otherwise, you'll reinforce the unhelpful fact that you're an out-of-towner.

And what's a Texas lawyer to do in a proceeding elsewhere? Again, if you're nimble, you'll probably adopt the standard pronunciation /vwahr **deer**/. Otherwise, you may come off as a rube. But if you have a strong regional accent for all your words, you might sound funny pronouncing only /vwahr **deer**/ like Webster. Use your judgment.

58. Master the use of the pause.

Perhaps the rhetorical device most undervalued and indeed ignored by lawyers is the pause. A strategic pause after an appropriate lead-in can add emphasis to whatever phrase or sentence immediately follows. It can also highlight the divisions of your argument. Instead of following the last sentence of your previous point with an immediate "I'd like to turn now to . . . ," insert a brief pause between the two. It will prepare your listeners for the transition that's to follow. It will also clarify the organization of your thoughts.

For a finer appreciation of this point, study the cadence of effective speakers—whether they're newscasters, professional commentators, or fellow lawyers. The good ones don't speak in a nonstop rat-a-tat-tat.

One specialized use of the pause is worth practicing: learn to stop talking whenever someone interrupts you. You will have to do this when a judge interrupts, and it is not a skill that comes naturally.

Preliminary Decision: Who Will Argue?

59. Send up the skilled advocate most knowledgeable about the case.

A client will sometimes press to have a "name" partner argue the case. Resist that pressure. Explain that the client best stands to win if the lawyer most familiar with the case (and, of course, skilled in oral advocacy) does the job. Every judge is familiar with the embarrassing and distracting spectacle of a senior lawyer at the rostrum butchering an appeal while a capable junior sitting at counsel table, more knowledgeable on the facts and law of the case, writhes in discomfort. The client may think the senior partner is doing a fine job, but the court knows better. And though the firm may please its client for the day by having its Big Name appear, over the long run that practice will cause the firm to lose more cases . . . and clients.

> "The attorney general of a state, the senior partner of a law firm, the head of a department, despite having done no work on the case in the lower court and being too busy to participate in the drafting of the brief, nonetheless 'designates' himself to argue the case. This advocate apparently thinks that an outward air of confidence and experience in a number of oral arguments are substitutes for a thorough understanding of this particular case."
> —Hon. William H. Rehnquist

In selecting counsel to argue an appeal, bear in mind that appellate advocacy and trial advocacy are different specialties. Some lawyers are good at both, just as some athletes excel in several sports. But skill in the one does not ensure skill in the other. So the lawyer who tried the case and who is, initially at least, the most knowledgeable on the facts, the proceedings below, and (perhaps) the law is not necessarily the best choice to argue. The same is true of the corporate counsel or narrow expert, who may be intimately familiar with the business that's the subject of the litigation but may lack the breadth of legal knowledge required to appreciate and explain the consequences of the client's position as it affects other fields.

60. Avoid splitting the argument between cocounsel.

When there are two counsel in the case, representing separate plaintiffs or defendants presenting the same issues, each one often wishes to argue. Avoid compromising by splitting the argument (if, by chance, the court would even allow it). Generally speaking, dividing the limited argument time between cocounsel produces two mediocre arguments instead of one excellent one. If counsel divide the argument by subject matter, the court is prevented from pursuing at greater length (and counsel from addressing at greater length) that aspect of the case in which the court has the greater interest. And if they don't divide it by subject matter, there will likely be two superficial treatments instead of one in-depth presentation. You disserve your client if you don't let the more capable and experienced lawyer do the whole job. If you cannot agree on which of the two of you that is, flip a coin. For good reason, most courts permit time-splitting only in rare cases.

The rare case in which time-splitting is appropriate arises when each of the two plaintiffs or defendants has a claim or defense that the other one does not share. Neither counsel would have any interest in, or knowledge about, the other's distinctive point. (When only one of them has a distinctive claim or defense, let that one make the whole argument.) The time should *not* be divided evenly; one or the other counsel should be allotted a small portion of the total time fairly devoted to that single point.

When the United States (or a state in a state-court case) has filed an amicus brief, it will sometimes offer to present oral argument if counsel for the side it is supporting will yield a portion of the argument time for that purpose. This is almost always a deal worth taking. While it shortens counsel's presentation time, it brings forcefully to the court's attention the interest of the government in the matter and adds to the case argument by unusually knowledgeable and experienced counsel.

When there is divided argument for the appellant, it is ordinarily the first speaker who reserves time for rebuttal. Remember to do so.

Months and Weeks Before Argument

61. Prepare assiduously.

The most difficult element of oral argument is the unexpected—the argument for your adversary or the question from the court that has not been anticipated. It's the supreme talent of the expert oral advocate (a talent that few possess) to be able to respond immediately and accurately to these surprises. But it is a basic skill of the competent oral advocate—and a skill we can all master—to ensure to the maximum extent possible that surprises don't occur.

This means thinking a lot about the case, turning it over in your mind, looking at it from various perspectives, racking your brain not only for the flaws in your adversary's case but also for the weaknesses of your own. It means preparing a defense for each of those weaknesses, even if it can be no more than an acknowledgment of its existence and the assertion that it's outweighed by other considerations. It means preparing for hundreds of different questions even though you may be asked only 20.

Develop the habit of making notes for argument while you're writing your briefs. Don't just hope you'll remember these thoughts: write them down and save them for the time when you'll be preparing for argument weeks or months in the future.

62. **Learn the record.**

An appeal is based on the record made in the lower court (or before an agency), and it's unprofessional to bring to the court's attention facts that are not found there. You will have done yourself harm rather than good if you stray beyond the record, only to be corrected (and implicitly chided) by opposing counsel. But the rule has an exception: if the court asks you a question relating to a fact not in the record, you should answer if the fact does not harm your case. Preface your response with, "It's not contained in the record, Your Honor, but my understanding is that . . . ." The court can stop you if it wants you to go no further.

As for facts *within* the record—including all the procedural doings below—your knowledge should be utterly complete and meticulously organized. Appellate judges rely on counsel for unique facts in the record much more than they do for the universally applicable (and hence usually familiar) points of law. Sorting out a procedural mess by pointing in the record to a particular clarifying action of the district court, or resolving an evidentiary dispute by citing the page in the record where the witness said precisely what your case requires—these responses can resolve the question conclusively, allowing the court (and you) to go on immediately to other aspects of the case. Of course, the most significant of these factual matters should have been

> "As familiarity with the record increases, its pages become old friends, checking out references becomes easier and quicker, and the feeling of confidence, of a strong grip on the case, grows immeasurably."
> —F. Trowbridge Vom Baur

addressed in your brief. But if the court thinks another fact pertinent—or is even just curious about another fact ("By the way, counsel, what was . . . ?")—only your mastery of the record will enable you to say what that fact is (or to say confidently that the fact is not known). You thus avoid wasting your argument time on speculation about the issue, and you sharpen the court's image of you as someone who really knows what this case is about.

Once again, a senior partner who is unfamiliar with the record and has no time to remedy that deficiency would be wise to let the junior partner who tried the case argue the appeal.

63. Learn the cases.

Presumably, your brief or reply brief will have distinguished your opponent's principal cases—and will have responded to your opponent's distinguishing of your own. Not only may the court wish to explore these disagreements, but it may have its own views of how and why the major cases cited or discussed are or are not germane. You must be able to enter these discussions with full and secure knowledge of the cases—their facts, their holdings, and their significant relevant dicta. Don't try to acquire such intimate knowledge of all the cited cases—just the principal ones, which would include all those actually discussed in either side's briefs. For the rest, you should have an alphabetized index showing their holdings, should the court inquire. It may be forgiven if you're unfamiliar with a new case injected into the controversy by the court itself or with a marginally relevant case cited in passing by one of the briefs. But it's inexcusable not to be armed to the teeth with regard to the cases that are central to the dispute.

The best way to learn the cases is to brief them in writing, just as you did in law school. What were the facts? What was the question decided? What was the holding? And what was the reasoning? Summarize these points *in your own words*: that is how you come to know cases—really know them. Then you can discuss them knowledgeably.

64. Decide which parts of your brief you'll cover.

Sometimes the time for your oral argument will be so limited that you can't do justice to all the points in your brief. When that is so, you shouldn't try to cover everything. Giving a lick and a promise to each point would just leave the court with the impression that your whole case is superficial and insubstantial. Instead, address your most important arguments in some depth. Tell the court at the outset that you'll be limiting your presentation in this fashion, though you are by no means abandoning your other points, for which you rest on your brief.

65. Be flexible.

Flexibility is the catchword for oral argument. Don't let the name "oral argument" deceive you. The opportunity to "argue" your case suggests that you will be able to make the points that you would like, in the order that you would prefer, and without interruption. If that is your view of the exercise, you will fare badly. In most courts, the modern oral argument would be more accurately described as a discussion led by the judges.

> "Some judges shoot the first question before the advocate has cleared his throat. Others hold their fire until the argument is well under way. The lawyer must be prepared to be told that the panel needs no oral recitation of the facts, to have the argument taken over completely by questions from the bench, and to find that the delivery of an entire argument is without a single question."
> —Hon. Murray I. Gurfein

Since you never know how assertively a judge or a panel of judges may intervene during your presentation, you must be prepared (1) to speak with almost no interruption from the bench, (2) to speak with a moderate number of questions, and (3) to speak with an almost uninterrupted stream of questions.

Approach the bench not with a set presentation in mind—not even a fixed outline of points in the order in which you wish to make them. Rather, stand up with a list of five to seven points that you want to make, and with a sure plan of how you intend to present each of them. But the order in which you present them, the amount of time you devote to each, and even whether you reach all the points or just the first several, will depend on what the judges want to discuss and at what length. It's up to you to turn the discussion, when you can, to each of the principal points you have in mind.

When a question from the court takes you forward to a subject you had planned to address later, you can hardly say, "Your Honor, I will come to that in a few minutes."

You jump ahead in your presentation to address that point at once and adjust the remainder accordingly. You must be adaptable enough—and the outline of your various presentations must be clear enough—to accomplish this.

66. Be absolutely clear on the theory of your case.

Judges are concerned not only with the outcome of your case but also with the outcome of the many future cases that will be governed by the rule you are urging the court to adopt. Indeed, in appellate courts—especially those with discretionary jurisdiction—the effect on future cases is their main focus. So it's an essential part of your argument to show that the rule of law you propose produces fair and reasonable results—not just in the present case, but in all cases to which it applies. If you fail to persuade the court of this, you will lose.

It is this interest of the court in the overall consequences of your proposed rule that produces the bane of the ill-prepared or dull-witted oral advocate: the hypothetical question. You should expect to receive a number of these. It is impossible to predict their precise content, and only absolute clarity about the theory of your case will enable you to provide an on-the-spot answer.

A good moot court before argument should have anticipated the most likely hypotheticals. Even if you've never

> "[T]here is in every case a cardinal point around which lesser points revolve like planets around the sun, or even as dead moons around a planet; a central fortress which if strongly held will make the loss of all the outworks immaterial."
> —John W. Davis

considered them before, however, the answer should be obvious if you truly know the theory of your case. Don't run away from the logical consequences of your theory. If, in a particular hypothetical situation, your theory produces a result that is seemingly unfair or unreasonable, explain why in reality that is not so; or, if that will not work, why the situation is so rare and freakish that it should not drive the governing rule; or, if all else fails, how an exception to the rule can be crafted for that highly unusual situation.

67. Be absolutely clear on the mandate you seek.

The judges we've consulted say that it's lamentably common for lawyers not to know how to fill in this blank: "The Court therefore orders that _____."
To supply what's missing, you must think through exactly what you're asking the court to do. Put it in the prayer of your brief.

Just as good lawyers begin their pleadings by consulting the pattern jury instructions so that they'll know what ultimately needs to be proved, they also begin preparing for a motion or appeal by crafting the order that will follow. If they want a temporary restraining order against a disaffected former employee, they don't just ask for an order "restraining Hef Helfenbein from disturbing company operations." Instead, they fashion a highly particularized order that's easier to enforce and hence more likely to be adopted: "Hef Helfenbein is restrained from (1) coming within 200 feet of the Goodyear plant; (2) telephoning any employee of Goodyear while that employee is on the job; (3) e-mailing any employee of Goodyear at a work e-mail address; (4) contacting any Goodyear supplier with whom he formerly had contact or knew about while he was a Goodyear employee; and (5) taking any other action designed to hamper or obstruct the company's operations."

If you think things through that thoroughly, you'll figure out a way to defend each of the measures you're requesting.

68. Organize and index the materials you may need.

Just like dead time on the radio, dead time in oral argument is a disaster. Fumbling through papers during an embarrassing silence not only wastes your argument time; it makes you look like an incompetent. All the materials you are likely to need—not just to support your presentation but to respond to arguments by the other side or questions from the court—should be methodically indexed and tabbed for ready access. This includes at least the critical testimony below, the record of proceedings below, the relevant pages of the important cases you or your opponent relies on, and the sections of statutes, portions of legislative history, and regulations you or your opponent relies on.

> "I speak from the fullness of my heart when I say that I have seen more trouble in Court over disorderly papers than from any other cause. So I decline to treat as a triviality beneath counsel's notice this matter of the tidiness and accessibility of the documents in the case."
> —Rt. Hon. Lord Macmillan

69. Conduct moot courts.

No preparation for oral argument is as valuable as a moot court in which you're interrogated by lawyers as familiar with your case as the court is likely to be. Nothing, absolutely nothing, is so effective in bringing to your attention issues that have not occurred to you and in revealing the flaws in your responses to issues you have been aware of.

If possible, assemble a panel of three inquisitors—and a diverse panel, not a claque. For example, if you're representing an environmental organization, don't put environmentalists on the panel. If you're representing an insurance company, avoid insurance-defense lawyers. In other words, try to find panelists who are unlikely to be sympathetic to your positions. Encourage them in advance to oppose your positions and to develop good hypotheticals. If you can find such accommodating friends and associates, have them read the briefs beforehand; at least be sure that they are well familiar with the issues.

Doing a moot court properly means staging it as though it's the real thing. Follow court decorum precisely, and if possible use a law-school or law-firm courtroom. Don't fall out of character and talk to the panelists as though they're not judges. Have a timer—though if you're preparing for only a ten-minute argument you would be well advised to let the moot court go on much longer. Indeed, it may always be desirable to go through the process twice—the first time lasting until the panel runs out of questions, and the second with the court's time limits imposed.

Finally, if at all possible, videotape the proceedings. Nothing can so convincingly persuade you of your mistakes as watching them.

70. Watch some arguments.

Professional speakers typically like to get an advance look at the room where they'll be speaking. They want to become familiar with its general dimensions, sample its acoustics, and generally get to feel comfortable in the space. The same goes for lawyers, who are professional speakers in courtrooms.

> "If you have to appear in a Tribunal or Court—in any capacity—familiarize yourself as best you can with its style, procedures, and atmosphere. Take time to sit in on someone else's troubles before your own are reached. And if in doubt about the ways and customs of the court or the idiosyncrasies of the Bench—ask the usher or the clerk. The more humble the official and the more distinguished the questioner, the more flattered he is likely to be."
> —Greville Janner

Make it a rule to watch proceedings in the courtroom where you'll be speaking. This means arriving for out-of-town hearings a day early.

Such "advancing" of your argument not only makes the room familiar. It also gives you a sense of the tribunal and its culture. It enables you to learn useful information by chatting with the clerk of court, the court reporter, or the bailiff. And it develops a feeling of ease and familiarity with the court's ways. If you happen to see the judge chastise counsel for sitting with an arm draped across the back of a bench—and some judges do this—you'll be glad you came and watched.

71. On the eve of argument, check your authorities.

How embarrassing to learn from the court that one of your leading cases has been reversed on appeal or overruled! That should never happen.

> "One of the most interesting cases I ever saw argued was a U.S. Sixth Circuit case in which both attorneys were arguing about the application of a case that had been overturned. When Judge Wellford finally asked one of the attorneys (who happened to be representing himself) whether he knew that the case was no longer good law, he responded (with great composure): 'No, Your Honor, but I would point out that opposing counsel didn't know it either.'"
> —Ronald J. Rychlak

A day or two before a scheduled oral argument, update your research. (Or have a junior colleague or trusted, well-trained paralegal do it.) See whether the courts have handed down any new decisions bearing on your case. Ensure that no pivotal cases have been overturned. Check also the principal authorities on which your adversary has relied. Use the most up-to-date, efficient research tools at your disposal. You must be as current on the relevant law as anyone else in the courtroom.

Before You Speak

72. Arrive at court plenty early with everything you need.

The proper frame of mind for making an oral argument is calm concentration. A last-minute, frenetic rush to the courthouse isn't conducive to this attitude. You'll have enough cause for nervousness without adding to it concern about arriving late. So leave with plenty of time to spare. In fact, if you're arguing the second case that day, be there for the first. Even if you've seen this particular panel in action before, it will help to get a feel for how they're functioning that day.

If you make it possible for something to go wrong, it will. So exclude the possibility. Make allowance for traffic delays and for misdirected luggage; learn in advance whether the courtroom requires an extension cord for your slide projector or an easel for your sketch of the accident scene. Know what you need, and have it at the courthouse well before you go on.

73. Make a good first impression. Dress appropriately and bear yourself with dignity.

Before you utter a word, you will convey to the court that you consider (or do not consider) this a serious occasion and that you entertain (or do not entertain) respect for the dignity of the tribunal. Consider your attire: Shakespeare wrote that "Apparel oft proclaims the man." If it does not do that, it at least proclaims the man's (or woman's) attitude toward the occasion. Don't show up in a sport jacket. Even if you're a man with long hair in a ponytail (and unless it's part of your special cultural heritage, we don't recommend this coiffure if advocacy before elderly judges is your day job), wear a dark suit (dark blue, dark gray, or black—not Tyrolean green or chocolate brown). The same for women—a dark, conservative suit. Wear a white shirt and a dark-red or blue tie. Nothing loud. Straighten your tie, comb your hair, and throw out your gum before you enter the courtroom.

> "You will not be stopped from arguing if you wear a race-track suit or sport a rainbow necktie. You will just create a first impression that you have strayed in at the wrong bar."
>
> —Hon. Robert H. Jackson

When you're waiting for your case to be heard, avoid reading newspapers or other materials not directly related to your case.

When your case is called, approach the counsel table in a brisk, businesslike manner—this is no time to joke or horse around with cocounsel. Sit erect, eyes fixed on the court, with the closest you can manage to an expression of sober anticipation.

74. Seat only cocounsel at counsel table.

The client will sometimes ask to attend oral argument —a request that today can hardly be denied. But don't seat the client beside you at counsel table. Clients have a tendency to whisper suggestions in your ear, or to display approval or disapproval of the proceedings by their expressions or mannerisms. Even if this doesn't distract you, it will distract the court. Seating the client in the audience is perfectly acceptable.

It is helpful to have cocounsel (perhaps a junior colleague) with you at counsel table. When you rise from your seat next to the lectern to speak, cocounsel slips into your chair so as to be able to pass you any materials needed during the argument. Tell cocounsel never to pass you a note while you are on your feet, except in an emergency—for example, if you have advised the court incorrectly about the contents of the record.

75. Bear in mind that even when you're not on your feet, you're onstage and working.

There is no rest time in an oral argument, for any of the counsel. When you are not speaking, pay close attention to the argument of opposing counsel so that you can respond to any new points or new emphases. Listen to the questions the court asks, and consider how you would answer (you may have to). Be careful, however, not to display reaction to opposing counsel's argument, as by shaking your head, rolling your eyes, smiling derisively, or otherwise registering disagreement. Maintain a dignified and respectful countenance, and calmly take notes. Similarly, when the court asks opposing counsel a question, don't display your answer by nodding or shaking your head. Laugh only when the court laughs (and, for that matter, weep when it weeps).

76. Approach the lectern unencumbered; adjust it to your height; stand erect and make eye contact with the court.

Approach the lectern in a brisk but unhurried manner. Don't come laden with books and papers: Lengthy materials that you need for quotation in argument, or for response to questions, should be ready at hand—perhaps on a nearby table—but should not be toted to the lectern.

We recommend that you approach the lectern with a single manila folder with no papers inside. Instead, write your bare-bones notes inside the folder itself, perhaps with the most telling record references listed. If you're overcome by brain-freeze, a glance at your notes should jog your mind. And since you have no loose papers inside, there'll be no risk of dropping papers onto the floor. The manila folder has the added advantage of closing up, so that others won't be privy to your notes as they lie on the counsel table.

> "There is something psychologically persuasive about a man who comes before an appellate court unburdened by a lot of legal paraphernalia."
>
> —H. Graham Morison

If you've taken the trouble to view the courtroom beforehand, you'll know whether the lectern is adjustable, and if so how. It is important that you fix it, if possible, to a comfortable height, not only because that makes it easier for you to consult your notes while you speak, but also because that may make it easier for the court to hear: the height of the microphone is often adjusted with the lectern.

Stand erect. Pause briefly before you open your mouth. Make eye contact with the judge or judges. Better to skip the smile, which may come across as nervous or condescending.

Substance of Argument

77. Greet the court and, if necessary, introduce yourself.

Make eye contact with the presiding judge and begin your presentation with whatever formulary introduction is customary in the court before which you're appearing. Typically it is "May it please the court." In the Supreme Court of the United States, it is "Mr. Chief Justice, and may it please the Court."

If the court has called you forward by name, proceed at once to your argument. If the court has merely said something like "Counsel for the appellant may proceed,"

> "It is a pleasingly brief and ritualistic touch to open with 'May it please the Court'; it is a crashingly boring waste of time to describe sycophantically how happy counsel is to be there."
>
> —Edward L. Lascher

begin by introducing yourself: "I am John Smith, representing the appellant, Paul Jones." Don't waste time describing your client unless you have reason to believe that the court has not read the briefs. In the latter event, state briefly the business or office of your natural-person client if that is relevant to the case ("Mr. Jones is the sheriff of Maricopa County, New Mexico") or the state of incorporation and business of your corporate client ("Ajax is a Delaware corporation that manufactures paper clips").

78. Have your opener down pat.

Anyone who has done public speaking knows that the hardest part is the opener. Your adrenaline is pumping. You're trying to keep nervousness out of your voice and manner, to establish eye contact with your audience, and to project a steady, even tone. This is no time to worry about what you're going to say. For this part of your presentation, commit your words to memory (though try not to deliver them as though by rote). Even for the opener, however, don't read from a prepared text.

Your opening should usually consist of, or at least contain, a brief outline of the subjects you intend to address: "I hope to discuss this morning first why this court has jurisdiction, then why the trial court's finding of negligence was unsupported, and finally why the damages awarded are plainly excessive." You should be under no illusion that you will actually get to reach all these subjects—that ultimately depends on the court (which is why you should put your strongest point first). But setting forth at the outset the full range of what you hope to address may induce the judges to make their questions more concise.

79. If you're the appellant, reserve rebuttal time.

It's never wise to waive rebuttal in advance—but it won't be given to you if you've used up all your time in your first presentation. In many courts, it's customary for counsel to request rebuttal time at the outset of an argument, right

> "Never waive rebuttal in advance, which means always be sure you have enough time left to rebut; otherwise, the appellee's lawyer may try to pull the wool over the judge's eyes knowing that you will not be able to correct his misstatements. But if, having reserved time for rebuttal, you find that you have nothing to say, perhaps because it is obvious that your opponent has said nothing to move the judges, then waive rebuttal rather than wasting the judges' time."
> —Hon. Richard A. Posner

after any personal introduction. In other courts, rebuttal time must be arranged with the courtroom deputy before argument. If you don't request or arrange it, you won't get it.

If the court has warning lights, find out from the clerk in advance whether they'll be set to take account of your reserved time. If not, you'll have to keep track of it yourself; if you use up all your time, your request for rebuttal will be dead.

80. Decide whether it's worth giving the facts and history of the case.

You have a limited time for argument, and don't want to waste a minute of it. If you're the appellant before a court that you believe may not have pored over your brief, or a court that assigns the opinion before argument (so that two of the three-judge panel may not have prepared as intensively as you would like), it may be worth your time to state the facts and history of the case, including, of course, the precise holding of the court below. In argument before a federal court of appeals, that would ordinarily be a waste of time: assume a basic knowledge of the facts and history, and proceed directly to your points of law. In your legal argument, of course, you can and should mention the specific facts that militate in favor of the outcome you're advocating.

If you're the appellee, and the appellant has already gone into the facts and history, *never repeat them*. Address only those points you wish to contest rather than burying them in a rehash of the whole story. This advice differs from what we recommend for the statement of facts in appellees' briefs (see p. 96) because (1) oral-argument time is more precious than briefing space, and (2) if you have followed our advice, the court will have had the opportunity to read your "take" on the facts in your brief. If the appellant has fully stated the facts in oral argument, you might say: "Our description of the salient facts is of course quite different from what you have heard today from appellant. But for that I will rest on our brief, except for making the following corrections to appellant's statement . . . ." If the appellant has not set forth the facts and history, you can usually omit them as well; any elements central to your case can be brought forth in your substantive argument.

81. If you're the appellant, lead with your strength.

Whereas in brief-writing it's often necessary to give logically prior points the first place, at oral argument you need not do so. Put your strongest point of law first. Never mind the logical order. By beginning with your best argument, you put your case in perspective: "Your Honors, we have four points in our brief, and we think they all merit your attention. But the utterly decisive point, and the one I would like to address first, is this: . . . ."

There is, of course, a second reason to begin with your strongest point: the court's questioning may hold you on that first point for all or most of your argument. If you save your best point for later, you may never reach it. And you don't want to spend most of your argument on your *opponent's* favored territory.

82. If you're the appellee, take account of what has preceded, clear the underbrush, and then go to your strength.

Argument for the appellee must be adaptable. What it should contain depends to a large extent on what the appellant has said and how favorably the court has received it. You may have to correct errors in the appellant's statement of the facts, and you may want to recast in your own terms the issue presented. The appellant's substantive points that have met with stiff resistance can be touched on lightly or, indeed, not at all.

An appellant's points that have been warmly received, however, or that are inherently strong, must be answered at the outset, espe-

"[T]he real mistake most respondent's counsel make is to have a speech prepared. It is a mistake to stand up and begin as if thirty minutes of oral argument did not just happen. This indicates that the respondent's counsel has not paid any attention to the petitioner's argument. There have been sixty questions asked, sixty questions answered, all kinds of things have happened, the case is in a complete disarray, and this guy starts off telling them what the question before the Court is. The Justices already know what the question is. I can guarantee that."
—Carter G. Phillips

cially if they are points that render your principal argument academic. You must "make space" for the court's acceptance of your argument by eliminating these prior impediments. If the court has been nodding in agreement with the appellant's contention that there is no jurisdiction, or that your principal point has been waived by failure to raise it below, the judges aren't going to pay very close attention to a merits argument that they think is academic. You must first rebut those antecedent arguments. An active panel will interrupt you to ask for such rebuttal, but you should have enough sense to begin with it on your own.

After that, your order of battle is just like that of the appellant: begin with your strength, and logical order be damned.

83. Avoid detailed discussion of precedents.

Whereas a full description of principal cases is often desirable in the brief, it is rarely worth the scarce time in oral argument. Stress what the cases hold, but go into their details only if the court inquires. When discussing cases cited in your brief, don't bother to give the citations—just the case names.

84. Focus quickly on crucial text, and tell the court where to find it.

"[L]et the court see—and I mean 'see'—the exact language with which they have to deal. Tell them, right at the beginning: 'The statutory language involved appears at page 4 of my brief. Though the clause is a somewhat long one, the issue turns, I believe, on the proper construction or effect of the words in two lines near the top of the page.' Give the court time to find the two lines, and then read the words to them."

—Erwin N. Griswold

If the outcome of your case hinges on the meaning of a text—whether statute, regulation, ordinance, or contractual provision—move quickly to consideration of that text. It greatly facilitates comprehension if the listener can read the text during the discussion. At the very outset, refer the court to the page in your brief where the text appears.

85. Don't beat a dead horse. Don't let a dead horse beat you.

When it's pretty clear that the court has been persuaded on your point, go on to the next one. Most counsel observe this rule but fail to observe its corollary: when it is clear that the court will not be persuaded on your point, move on. Otherwise-capable advocates often insist on tenaciously pressing and pressing a point that the court is vigorously resisting and will obviously not accept. Tenacity is good, but use some judgment. You have limited time, and it's foolish to waste it on a lost cause. Go on to something else.

86. Stop promptly when you're out of time.

When the red light comes on, or when you are otherwise informed that your time is up, take at most five or ten seconds to finish your sentence and prepare to sit down. Don't look yearningly at the presiding judge as if requesting more time. Don't announce regretfully (much less resentfully) that it looks as if your time has run out. Rarely will judges relent to those unsubtle suggestions, and when they do they will resent the imposition. Bad note to end on.

87. When you have time left, but nothing else useful to say, conclude effectively and gracefully.

The time allotted for oral argument is typically so short that a concluding summary of your remarks, going back over all your principal points, is neither necessary nor possible. The exception to this may be the conclusion to the appellant's rebuttal. In any event, just in case you're confronted with a "cold" bench and end up with plenty of time, you should have a prepared 30-second summary in mind. Instead of a summary, if you have a truly unanswerable point that is fatal to your adversary's case, you might consider concluding your main presentation or rebuttal with a zinger—pointing out (politely) that no coherent response has been forthcoming.

Whether or not you have time for a summary or a zinger, you should at least conclude with a graceful ending rather than just trailing off into silence. Something like: "For the reasons we have discussed, Your Honors, fairness demands

> "[I]n one case petitioner's lawyer took such a battering from the court that it was obvious to everyone the judgment below would be affirmed. Counsel for the respondent arose, bowed, and said, 'If the Court please, I must apologize for an error in my brief. At page 32, second line from the bottom, the citation should be to 112 Federal Second and not to 112 Federal.... Unless there are any questions, I will submit the respondent's case on the brief,' and sat down. I have it on excellent authority that it was one of the most effective arguments ever heard by that court."
> —Frederick Bernays Wiener

and the law requires compensation for the appellant's injury. We ask that you affirm the judgment of the court of appeals."

What about a thank-you after that? Not all judges care about it (they're just doing their job, after all), but none are offended and some appreciate it.[48] So why not? Don't overdo it, however. Shun a treacly, fawning expression such as, "Thank you, Your Honors, for your time and close attention this afternoon." Yuck. A simple two-word "Thank you" is fine.

To rush from the lectern would suggest that you have not thoroughly enjoyed the experience, an impression you don't wish to convey. Calmly, deliberately close up your notes and take your seat.

---

48 *See* Arthur L. Alarcon, "Points on Appeal," in *Appellate Practice Manual* 95, 101 (Priscilla Anne Schwab ed., 1992) (noting that "[s]urprisingly few lawyers" say "thank you" at the end).

88. Take account of the special considerations applicable to rebuttal argument.

The advice not to waive rebuttal in advance is not much needed. But the advice to use only so much as is necessary (including none at all) is rarely heeded. What is true of your main presentation is true of rebuttal as well: what doesn't help hurts because it distracts attention from the rest. Even if you have a large chunk of rebuttal time available, don't use it to address insignificant details. Hit the major points that need repair, and sit down. And if the other side has not laid a glove on you, and the court is obviously in your corner, leave well enough alone. Utter those words—always welcome to judicial ears—that powerfully display your confidence in your case and ingratiate you to the court by giving the judges a couple more minutes for lunch: "Unless the court has further questions, we waive our rebuttal."

Like the reply brief, rebuttal argument is for *rebuttal*. It has two purposes, and two purposes only: (1) responding to significant new points raised for the first time in the appellee's oral presentation; and (2) responding to the appellee's significant oral attacks on your oral presentation or your brief. Don't use it merely to rehash your affirmative points (except, if time is

> "The carefully made rebuttal can be extremely helpful in leaving the Court with its focus not on the last words of your adversary but on the striking point that you believe to be most in your favor. The rebuttal should never be prepared in advance. You should make notes during the respondent's (or appellee's) argument, and then, just before he sits down, strike for discussion everything except the one or two points which are most helpful to your cause."
> —E. Barrett Prettyman Jr.

available, in a brief concluding summary) or to introduce an affirmative point you left out of your principal argument. If it was dispensable there, it is dispensable here. And never, ever use it to introduce a brand-new point. This sharp practice the court may well remark on.

The most important task in rebuttal is to respond to any significant new point raised in the appellee's presentation— that is, a significant point that you had no opportunity to confront in your brief or in oral argument. This will be your only chance to reply.

Avoid the temptation of scattershot argument. Many lawyers who carefully pick their targets in their briefs and principal oral presentations stand up for rebuttal and shoot at everything in sight—going down the points of error they have jotted down during the appellee's presentation. But the scattershot approach is no more effective here than anywhere else. While you're jotting down your notes, consider which of them is worth the trouble to discuss and how those relatively few points can be effectively organized. This is multitasking under pressure, but it is essential.

Because rebuttal must be prepared under such pressure, give it some advance thought. You know from the appellee's brief what's likely to be thrown at you. Think about which arguments it might be better to leave unaddressed in your principal argument and to come down hard on in rebuttal.

While a summary of main points is not ordinarily worth the time at the end of the principal oral presentations, by the time you stand up for rebuttal the court has listened to the appellee for a long time, and your main points are far in the past. If the time is available, it would be well to go over them quickly, at the conclusion of your remarks. It's best to omit that, however, if you already gave a summary at the end of your principal argument; besides being boring, repeated summaries display a certain lack of confidence in the judges' short-term memory.

Manner of Argument

89. Look the judges in the eye. Connect.

Everyone who speaks in public has heard—and most have learned—that it is a blunder to bury your head in notes. You must look up. But that is not enough. Many speakers look up at some indeterminate spot on the back wall or on the ceiling. Even with a large audience, that's no good. But especially when you're standing in court, look at the judge. In the eye. That's the only way to establish the relationship you want. You are advising the judge, not merely speaking in the same room.

Ah, but what if the court has more than one judge? Which of them should you favor? Some advocates fix their gaze constantly on the presiding judge, in the center of the bench. Big mistake. Even a presiding judge who happens to be a chief judge or chief justice is going to cast just one vote in the case, the same as the other members of the panel. All the other judges will, for most of the time at least, be looking at you, and you don't want to give them the impression that you are intent on persuading only the chief. Return their gaze, looking from

> "Lawyer A, a fine attorney from a recognized Wall Street, N.Y., firm, didn't look the court in the eye once, but delivered his entire argument looking down at his notes. Unfortunately for him, the wooden podium casts no vote in the conference."
>
> —Hon. Myron H. Bright

judge to judge as though each of them is the object of your solicitude—as indeed each of them should be.

There is one exception to this general rule: when you're responding to a question from the bench, look at the judge who asked it. You want to convey to that questioner that you are making a genuine effort to answer the inquiry—which you will not do if you are looking about at the questioner's colleagues while you deliver your answer.

An error almost as common as looking at (and thus seeming to address) only the presiding judge is the tendency to speak to and look at only the judge who is giving you a hard time. Even if the other members of the panel are silent, do not assume that their silence indicates that they already agree with you and need no persuasion. Unless you're answering a question, look from one member of the court to another, making it clear that you're speaking to all of them.

90. Be conversational but not familiar.

Remember the relationship you want to establish: that of a junior partner addressing a senior partner. Speak accordingly—not being obsequious or excessively deferential, nor being offhand or chummy.

It's helpful to refer to the judges by name when answering their questions—Judge Smith, Judge Jones, etc. The game is not worth the candle, however, if you're no good at names and are liable to call Smith "Jones." "Your Honor" will do just fine. A worse mistake, of course, is to mispronounce the name of a judge. Make sure you have that right.

Avoid the temptation to show off by attributing cases raised during your argument to their sitting authors. ("As Justice Smith wrote for the Court in *Doe v. Roe*, ...") The named judges will not be flattered and may well resent your trying to tie them down to earlier opinions. If they care about the consistency of their holdings, they (or their law clerks) will be well aware of their earlier commitments. The personal reference, if it has any purpose other than flattery, suggests an unseemly belief that judges on that bench adhere less faithfully to precedents written by others.

> "The judicial process will have approached perfection when the discussion between judges and lawyer is as free and natural as that between persons, mutually respecting each other, who try to explain their points of view for their common good."
> —Piero Calamandrei

91. Use correct courtroom terminology.

Address the members of the court correctly. Don't call a justice a judge, or a judge a justice. Give the chief judge or chief justice the correct title. Chief Justice Rehnquist used to correct counsel in mid-argument if they referred to him as "Justice Rehnquist." Even judges who don't correct you will notice and keep in mind that you are careless.

An allied point: The words to be used in addressing a judge without stating his or her name are "Your Honor." "Judge" or "Justice" alone is a slightly inferior substitute; "Sir" or "Ma'am" much inferior. Many judges will take no offense whatever at any of these substitutes; but some will.

Be aware also of the regional variations in legal terminology. For example, the Supreme Court in New York State is a trial court, and the highest court is the Court of Appeals. In California, the intermediate court is the Court of Appeal, not the "Court of Appeals." In Illinois it's the Illinois Appellate Court, there being no "Illinois Court of Appeals." The United States Court of Appeals for the District of Columbia Circuit is quite different from the District of Columbia Court of Appeals. And so on.

Trivialities, you say? No. It's a matter of legal literacy. Using the wrong term displays an ignorance of legal practice, which makes you less credible.

92. Never read an argument; never deliver it from memory except the opener and perhaps the closer.

Some court rules outright prohibit the reading of an argument. Even where it's not prohibited, it's frowned on. In the Supreme Court of the United States, the Chief Justice has been known to interrupt counsel who appeared to be reading.

And of course it makes no sense to read. Remember the relationship you're trying to establish. What would you think of an associate who came into your office to discuss a case and read from a typed sheet? Would you think it was worth kicking the case around with that lawyer?

Committing an argument to memory (except for the opener) is almost as bad. Your audience can tell—and it makes you seem to be not advising and reasoning with the court, but talking at it. Memorization has the added disadvantage of leaving you at sea once your set spiel has been interrupted by a series of questions. Memorize the preferred sequence of your ideas, and approach the lectern with no more than a few outlined points.

93. Treasure simplicity.

Express your ideas in a straightforward fashion, not circuitously—and in plain words. When you describe events, treat them chronologically.

Avoid pretentious expression. You're trying to get judges to understand a case, not to impress them with your erudition. Your job is to make a complex case simple, not to make a simple case sound complex. This end is best achieved by clear thoughts simply expressed.

Part of simplicity is brevity. Get to the point. Don't meander in leading up to it or embellish it once made. Every fact, every observation, every argument that does not positively strengthen your case positively weakens it by distracting attention.

94. Don't chew your fingernails.

All right, we have never actually seen attorneys chewing their fingernails at oral argument. But we have seen just about every other distracting and annoying sort of mannerism. Some appear to be unconscious and unintended: drumming one's pencil on the counsel table, swaying back and forth during argument, fixing one's gaze on the lectern or off into the middle distance instead of looking at the judge who is asking a question, fiddling with papers on the lectern, going through the argument with a frozen smile that's either silly or supercilious. Work to identify and eliminate these unintended distractions.

Other mannerisms (worse still) seem quite calculated: punctuating a telling statement by leaning forward over the lectern or poking at the air with one's pencil, striking a pose of deep contemplation by removing one's glasses and nibbling at the end of the earpiece, repeatedly putting one's glasses on and off with an audible clack and using them as a gesticulating prop, occasionally stepping away from the lectern to one side or the other. These pieces of stage business, probably originating in the Actor's Workshop, are very effective in keeping a Rumpole of the Bailey audience entertained. But they do nothing but annoy and distract the judge who is trying hard to concentrate on the factual and legal details of a complicated case. Stand up straight and speak your piece. If you would not be surprised to hear the courtroom applaud when you sit down, you have overacted.

95. Present your argument as truth, not as your opinion.

Avoid the first-person singular (*I, me*) and such constructions as "Appellant contends that . . . ," "It is our position that . . . ," "In our view . . . ." All of these usages make what you want to present as truth and fact seem like merely your own or your client's idea. And use of the first person also makes you sound full of yourself. Tell the judges what the law is, not what you think it to be.

96. Never speak over a judge.

As soon as a judge begins to speak—even if it's a rude interruption—stop speaking. In midsentence, if necessary. Not only does this display appropriate respect for the court, but the stark interruption of your presentation will cause most judges to interject their questions at more appropriate times later in your argument.

"The Court is not your competitor. When one of the justices wants center stage, give it up. No matter how brilliant or how telling the point you are making, when one of the justices says something, you should stop talking and start listening."

—Rex E. Lee

It's surprising how many lawyers talk over the court. Some of them insist that they do no such thing, then listen incredulously to the tapes that show the contrary. Stopping at once when you yourself are being interrupted in midsentence is not a natural instinct. You must learn to do it.

Of course, some lawyers must be interrupted in midsentence if they are to be questioned at all. Some counsel have perfected the technique of catching their breath in midsentence, so that they can leave no pause between sentences and thus discourage interruptions. The technique is self-defeating. The judge will interrupt rudely if that's the only option you provide—and while waiting to pounce on a pause between sentences will be listening only to the sounds you're making and not to the thoughts you're trying to convey.

97. Never ask how much time you have left.

It's your job to keep track of the time, not the court's. Many courts have a warning light that goes on about five minutes before the deadline, and then a red light when time is up. Whether or not such a device exists, you should place your own watch on the lectern and keep track of the passing minutes. Don't, by the way, keep looking up at the big clock that hangs above the bench—especially not when the court is asking you a question.

98. Never (or almost never) put any other question to the court.

Needless to say, you should never put a substantive question to the court. You're there to answer, not to ask, and some judges may resent the role-reversal. Nor should you ever ask the court whether you've adequately answered a question. Do your best and move on. Otherwise you may find yourself consuming your time in a fruitless effort to persuade the court of a point on which it will not be persuaded.

> "A judge on the bench asks the advocate what he considers a very pertinent question. The latter, instead of undertaking to answer the query, says: 'Your Honor, let me ask you this question.' Personally, I think that is the most classic of all 'famous last words.' For an attorney to honestly believe that by such conduct in an oral argument he is still on the objective track of persuasion is fantastic."
> —Watson Clay

The only questions one would expect skillful counsel to ask are (1) whether counsel's understanding of a question is correct, and (2) whether the court has any further questions.

99. Be cautious about humor.

Never tell prepared jokes. They almost invariably bomb. In *Roe v. Wade*, an assistant attorney general for the State of Texas, who was arguing against two women lawyers, led with what he probably considered courtly Southern humor:

> Mr. Chief Justice, and may it please the Court. It's an old joke, but when a man argues against two beautiful ladies like this, they're going to have the last word.

186

No one laughed. Onlookers said that during an embarrassing silence, Chief Justice Burger scowled at the advocate.

As for uncanned humor, we have heard counsel with an easygoing sense of humor break the tension and foster amicable discourse by an unscripted witticism—always gentle and often self-deprecating. The problems are that (1) only someone with a genuinely good sense of humor, and a feel for when humor is appropriate, can pull this off; (2) many of us who think we have those qualities don't; and (3) some judges have no sense of humor. All in all, the benefit is not worth the risk. You should, of course, display restrained appreciation for any attempt at humor by the court.

100. Don't use visual aids unintelligently.

Generally speaking, visual aids are for jury trials. Judges will be offended by the schoolmarmish use of a chart and a pointer to drive home a point that can be made perfectly well in words. When you need visual reinforcement, resort first to the Appendix in your brief. That has the added advantage of remaining with the judge after the argument is over and the easel folded away. If, for example, the issue is whether there were sufficient contacts with the state to confer jurisdiction, a chart in the Appendix might list the many contacts contained in cases finding jurisdiction, compared with the few contacts contained in your case. That wouldn't work as a blown-up chart used in live court.

But sometimes visual aids are useful and proper. For example, when geography matters, as in a boundary dispute or election redistricting, the small detail shown in an Appendix can be greatly improved on with a full-size map that you can refer to during argument.

Handling Questions

101. Welcome questions.

In many modern courts, much less oral-argument time is spent in set-piece presentations by counsel than in back-and-forth discussions between counsel and court, prompted by questions from the judges. This is particularly likely in courts whose judges have had time to study the briefs carefully. Who wants to listen to an audiobook after reading the book itself? Given the very limited time available for oral argument, judges want to hear counsel's response to the questions that the brief has raised in their minds, rather than sit through a repetition of legal points on which they may already be persuaded. As never before, the ability to handle questions and to integrate answers into counsel's set presentation is an essential skill of the effective advocate.

Only the least competent counsel regards questions from the bench as an annoyance and distraction. What skillful and experienced counsel most fears is

> "As between courts that sit in sphinxlike silence and courts that unduly interrupt, my own preference is for the latter. Indeed, I believe that most appellate advocates favor questions from the bench."
>
> —Hon. Simon H. Rifkind

a "cold" bench, which leaves the advocate looking from face to face for some indication of interest, some hint about what aspects of the case a judge finds troubling. Ultimately, with no questions forthcoming, the lawyer is driven to simply regurgitating the brief. Less competent counsel considers this a relief; wise counsel considers it a disaster. The point is this: Only when you are responding to a question from the bench can you be sure that you are not wasting your time—pounding home a point on which the court is already entirely convinced or clarifying an issue on which the court is in no confusion.

Indeed, if you're not receiving any questions, it's a good idea to invite them—for example, by concluding one portion of your argument with "Unless the court has any questions on this point [pause], I will proceed to discuss the issue of _____."

Of course, even if you regard questions (or a particular question) as a waste of your valuable time, you should never *appear* to do so. Nothing is so annoying to a judge as counsel's stealing a glance upward at the court clock when a question is asked—as though thinking, "This fool is making me consume valuable time that I could be spending on repeating my brief!"

But to say that you must welcome every question is not to say that you must treat the good ones and the bad ones alike. As an experienced member of the Supreme Court bar advises, it's a bad mistake

> to take a question you very well know to be totally beside the point and treat it at great length simply because a Justice happened to ask it. Since you can never tell a Justice that his question is irrelevant, the only guideline I can give is that

counsel should answer such a question directly and courteously, but as quickly as possible.[49]

102. Listen carefully and, if necessary, ask for clarification.

Much argument time has been wasted by counsel's launching off into the answer to a question that is entirely different from the one the judge has posed. It sometimes takes minutes to identify and straighten out the misunderstanding. If you don't understand a question, ask politely that it be repeated. If you *think* you understand it but are not entirely sure, begin your response with something like: "If I understand your question correctly, you are asking whether . . . ." But don't damage your credibility by restating the question in a way that avoids the part of the question you'd have difficulty answering.

Listen closely also to the questions that the court asks your adversary—not only because you may get the same questions but also because the general line of inquiry discloses the judges' principal concerns, which you must be sure to address in your ensuing presentation.

> "If you are going to be able to intelligently answer a question, you must first listen to the question. . . . [I]t is surprising how often appellate advocates, just like many people in private conversation, seem to hear only part of the question, and respond to the part of it that they heard even though the answer they give may not be an adequate response to the entire question."
> —Hon. William H. Rehnquist

---

49 E. Barrett Prettyman Jr., *Supreme Court Advocacy: Random Thoughts in a Day of Time Restrictions*, Litig., Winter 1978, at 16, 18.

103. Never postpone an answer.

Perhaps the most annoying of all responses to a judge's question is this: "Your Honor, I'll get to that point later. First, ..." Go where the court wants you to go! Besides offending the court's dignity, you invite the judge to conclude (as most will) that you have no effective response. And you invite suspicion that the promised "later" will never come. (Justice John M. Harlan asserted that the usual result of a postponed answer was a never-addressed question.[50]) At the very least the questioner is distracted from your ensuing discussion, waiting eagerly for that to be done with and for the question to be addressed. As elegantly described by Ben W. Palmer, a Minneapolis practitioner of the mid-20th century, "everything you may say thereafter may be suspended in the air like a levitated body or more likely a corpse—the corpse of your dead case."[51]

When following our advice not to postpone an answer, refrain from saying something like "Your Honor, I was planning to address that point later on, but since you ask I shall come to it at once." Frankly, the court doesn't care a fig whether you were planning to address it later or not—you'll get no points for that even if the judges believe you. And the clear suggestion that the nasty ol' judge has ruined your orderly plan of presentation will not be well received. Just answer the question.

---

50 John M. Harlan, *What Part Does the Oral Argument Play in the Conduct of an Appeal?*, 41 Cornell L.Q. 6, 9 (1955).

51 Ben W. Palmer, *Courtroom Strategies* 205 (1959).

104. If you don't know, say so. And never give a categorical answer you're unsure of.

If you don't have the answer to a question, say so. Counsel are not expected to know everything—and even with regard to a point that they *should* know, acknowledged ignorance is better than proffered misinformation. If the point you don't know seems of great interest to the court, offer to submit a supplemental brief—perhaps a letter brief. Memorize these words: "I'm sorry, Your Honor, but I don't know the answer. I'll provide that information by letter this afternoon."

> "If you don't know the answer, admit it; the penalty for not having an answer at your fingertips is less severe than the penalty for trying to fake it, getting caught, and giving the court an opportunity to bat you around like a cat playing with a ball of yarn."
> —William J. Boyce

If you're in the least uncertain about your answer, qualify it. ("I believe, Your Honor, that the answer is yes, but I am not entirely sure.") The court will appreciate your honesty.

105. Begin with a "yes" or a "no."

Don't force the court to ask, when you are done answering a question, "Is that a 'yes' or a 'no'?" Begin with "yes" or "no" (not "maybe" or "sometimes"), and then follow with whatever qualification is necessary. "Yes, except that . . . ." "No, unless . . . ." You want an answer followed by an explanation, not an explanation followed by an answer. If the court tries to cut you off before the explanation, you can politely ask, "May I please explain my answer?" When the answer is seemingly

> "Nonresponsive and evasive answers merely invite the guillotine."
> —Hon. Thurgood Marshall

not favorable to your case, give it anyway—and then proceed to explain why it is not relevant or not significant. Don't run away from difficulties. Acknowledge and neutralize them.

106. Never praise a question.

Never—never—patronize a judge by volunteering "That's a very good question." Of *course* it is! *All* judges' questions are ex officio brilliant.

Nor should you express your delight at a judge's question. This was among Chief Justice Rehnquist's bêtes noires. Here's what he said: "[F]or heaven's sake, forget about the rather trite response 'I'm glad you asked that question' or 'That question goes to the very heart of the case.' We have all heard this response to our questions, and we are all a little bit skeptical about it."[52]

107. Willingly answer hypotheticals.

Many of the questions posed by an appellate panel will be so-called hypotheticals, inquiring how the rule of law you are urging will apply to a fact situation different from the one before the court. Don't display your low regard for the intelligence of the interrogator by beginning your response to an obvious hypothetical with "That is not this case." Of *course* it's not; that's why it's a hypothetical.

---

52 William H. Rehnquist, *Oral Advocacy*, 27 S. Tex. L. Rev. 289, 302 (1986).

You may consider some hypotheticals to be, so to speak, off the wall. And they may indeed be so. Answer them anyway: the judge expects an answer.

108. After answering, transition back into your argument—smoothly, which means not necessarily at the point where you left it.

Among the greatest of challenges for the oral advocate is achieving a graceful and orderly return to one of the points in the prepared presentation after answering a question. Grace and order suggest that the return should take the listener to a point closely related to the just-delivered answer and not to whatever point was next in the advocate's prepared outline. Some lawyers get defeated by the interruption of their set presentation and never recover. Others move cumbersomely back to their outline by saying, "Now if I could return to the point I was making a moment ago"—the implication being, "before Judge X interrupted me."

The literature on advocacy teems with expressions of the idea that you must be prepared to deliver the points of your argument in any possible order and to transition smoothly between them. Chief Justice Roberts used the following method to achieve that end when he was

> "Flexibility in an oral argument is ... absolutely indispensable. A fixed or prepared written argument is doomed. Your argument must adjust to the questioning of the court as well as your opponent's presentation. I must warn you that, without adaptability, your opportunity for persuasion will be a failure and neither you nor the court will learn anything of value from the exercise."
> —Hon. Irving R. Kaufman

in practice: he would summarize on separate index cards each of the four or five points essential to his presentation. Then he would repeatedly shuffle the deck and give the argument in the order in which the cards fell. In this way, he would devise seamless ways of moving from any point to any other point.

109. Recognize friendly questions.

Most questions you receive will be probing the weaknesses of your case. But not all of them. Occasionally, especially when you have been hard pressed by another member of the panel, a judge will try to give you a helping hand—asking, for example, a rhetorical question that suggests what your answer to an earlier hostile question might have been. It's the height of ingratitude (and of foolishness) to mistake this friendly intervention for a hostile one and to resist the help that has been offered.

> "Do not assume that the question is hostile. Many are. But some are neutral, and some are helpful. One example of a helpful question is a statement which, while framed as a question ('Is it your position that?' or 'Is it not true that?'), is actually a more persuasive argument than has come to your unassisted mind. Some questions are analogous to a lifeline extended to a drowning person."
> —Rex E. Lee

110. Learn how to handle a difficult judge.

You will sometimes encounter a judge whose questions are designed not to obtain enlightenment but to demonstrate to colleagues the weakness of your case. During your exchange with such a questioner, be sure to maintain eye contact. Don't display your discomfort by looking down at some imaginary text whence will come your redemption. Look the judge straight in the eye and continue responding in a professional, firm manner.

It's always a mistake to evade questions, but especially so when the question comes from a difficult judge. That judge will persist, and you'll end up spending even more time reasoning with someone who will not be persuaded. Confront the question squarely with your best answer, and try to move on.

Sometimes such a questioner, after you have answered as best you can, will continue to press the same point, even though (indeed, *because*) you are unable to say anything more. You must devise a polite, nonalienating way to end this exchange, or it will consume much of your argument time. After a decent amount of time has been spent on the point, it would be appropriate to say, "Your Honor, I cannot respond to your objection with anything other than what I have already said."

> "[T]he rule is a very simple one: with both good and bad judges, it is in your interest, and in the interests of your clients, to maintain fastidious politeness and an undiminished attitude of respect. Even if you think your judge is a rude, ill-educated boor, behave toward him or her with perfect courtesy. You'll accomplish nothing if you don't."
>
> —Keith Evans

A similar problem is presented when a judge's questions about one part of your presentation are so numerous that the time remaining for an important but yet-to-be-addressed portion is growing short. You must try, politely, to regain control of the subject matter. The court will not take it amiss if, after responding to one question, you continue quickly: "With the court's permission, I would like to turn now to . . . ."

Whatever else you do when confronted by a hostile and unreasonable judge, don't reply in kind. Don't become hostile yourself; don't display anger, annoyance, or impatience. Keep telling yourself that you owe it to your client—because you do.

Even so, lawyers are entitled to take great delight in the wonderful comeuppances to judicial boorishness that some of their more rash predecessors have devised. Our favorite was also a favorite of Justice Robert H. Jackson.[53] A noted barrister, F.E. Smith, had argued at some length in an English court when the judge leaned over the bench and said: "I have read your case, Mr. Smith, and I am no wiser than I was when I started." To which the barrister replied: "Possibly not, My Lord, but far better informed."[54] Smith, who later became a famous judge as the Earl of Birkenhead, could reportedly carry off such snappy rejoinders with impunity.[55] We doubt that, but in any case we don't recommend that you emulate him.

---

53 *See* Robert H. Jackson, *Advocacy Before the Supreme Court*, 37 ABA J. 801, 862 (1951).

54 The Second Earl of Birkenhead, *The Life of F.E. Smith, First Earl of Birkenhead* 99 (1959).

55 *Id.*

111. Beware invited concessions.

We've advised you to volunteer concessions that careful deliberation shows are necessary (§ 11). But concessions that you're pressed to make on horseback, at oral argument, are something else. The unduly accommodating lawyer—a frequently observed creature, especially in appellate courts—has given away many a case. The lawbooks are filled with affirmances that would have been reversals or remands for further proceedings were it not for the concession of a crucial fact by accommodating counsel. And propositions of law that might well have been exceedingly difficult for an opinion to establish have often been happily resolved (for purposes of the case at hand, at least) by foolish concessions.

> "Never be intimidated. Frequently, judges will ask, 'Of course, counselor, you will concede, won't you, that...?' Be very careful about answering this kind of question. It is hardly ever a friendly one. It is far better to say bravely that you will not concede an issue than to find out later that your concession, hastily made at oral argument, was the reason you lost.'"
> —Talbot D'Alemberte

Any judge who presses you for a concession might well use it against you. That judge may, for example, be testing the validity of your basic premise—or rather, the fidelity of your adherence to that basic premise. Let's say you're defending the lawfulness of an officer's traffic stop on the ground that there was an objectively valid basis for the stop, such as a broken taillight on the vehicle. Counsel for the defense contends that the stop was unlawful because the real reason for it was the officer's suspicion that the occupants of the car were drug-runners. You might get the following honey-

199

coated inquiry from the court: "Counsel, surely you would agree that an officer could not pull a car over—even a car with a broken taillight—solely for the purpose of harassing its occupants." What a wonderful opportunity for you to show that you are just as reasonable a person as this judge. But if you rise to this bait, you will have abandoned the fundamental premise of your case: that whatever the subjective motivation for a stop, it is validated by objective indication of probable cause. For being so accommodating, you can expect the court's opinion excluding the evidence derived in the traffic stop to read: "Counsel has acknowledged that the subjective intent of the arresting officer is relevant, and we see no difference between an invalidating intent to harass and an invalidating intent to search for drugs without probable cause."

It is not unusual for a judge to come to the bench, having read all the briefs, with a clear idea of what the judgment ought to be *but for* one missing fact, or *but for* one possible legal obstacle. If the judge can get you to concede that fact, or to concede a point that would make that legal obstacle irrelevant, the opinion is all but written. You should not cooperate in your own destruction.

After the Battle

112. Advise the court of significant new authority.

When argument is over, and the case is under advisement, your job is not quite done. Be on the lookout for significant new authority—a new governing case or a new statutory provision—that would have formed part of your argument had it existed earlier. Bring it to the court's attention by letter (with copy to opposing counsel, of course).[56] Two caveats: (1) Be sure the authority is new—i.e., became available postargument. This is not a device to plug the holes in your brief. (2) Be sure the authority is significant. You will lose points for bothering an appellate court with an additional lower-court case that came out your way.

113. If you're unhappy with the ruling, think about filing a motion for reconsideration.

Motions for reconsideration bear various titles. In federal district courts, for example, a motion for reconsideration of the judgment is called a "motion to alter or amend judgment,"[57] and in federal courts of appeals and the Supreme Court a "petition for rehearing."[58] It's hard to provide good advice about motions for reconsideration in the abstract,

---

56 *See* Fed. R. App. P. 28(j).

57 *See* Fed. R. Civ. P. 59(e).

58 *See* Fed. R. App. P. 40; Sup. Ct. R. 44.

outside the context of a particular court. In the Supreme Court of the United States, petitions for rehearing are rarely filed by paid counsel and are almost never granted, even on petitions for certiorari. You'd almost certainly be wasting your time and your client's money. In most other courts, however, motions for reconsideration are not unusual. One commentary calls them "routine" in federal courts[59]—a phenomenon that may have something to do with the fact that the pendency of such a motion extends the time for filing a notice of appeal or petition for writ of certiorari.[60] Statistics on the success of motions for reconsideration are hard to come by, and may not be very informative anyway, since there is almost certainly great variation from court to court. Suffice it to say that your chances of success are slim.[61] They'll be better (but still not good) if you limit your motions as we suggest below.

One ground that always makes a motion to reconsider a merits ruling appropriate, and is indeed welcomed by the court, is a subsequent decision from a governing authority showing the court's judgment or ruling to be in error. The court is no more eager to be reversed on appeal than you are eager to incur the expense of an appeal. Short of that,

---

59 David Giles & Bruce Brown, *Rehearing Motions: The Switch of Minds That Saved the Times*, Litig., Winter 1999, at 48, 65.

60 *See* Fed. R. App. P. 4(a)(4); Sup. Ct. R. 13(3).

61 *See* Craig T. Enoch & Michael S. Truesdale, *Issues and Petitions: The Impact on Supreme Court Practice*, 31 St. Mary's L.J. 565, 574 n.33 (2000) (putting the rate of success in Texas appellate courts at "below 6%"); Antone E. Turley, *Preserving Your Right to Appeal*, Nat'l Bus. Inst., 31533 NBI-CLE 118, 181 (2006) (putting the rate in Ohio appellate courts at 2%).

however, it's wise to adhere to the standard of Rule 40 of the Federal Rules of Appellate Procedure, which requires the motion for reconsideration to explain the points that, in the movant's opinion, the court has "overlooked or misapprehended." If the judgment or order mentions your point, understands it, and rejects it, a motion for reconsideration will be useless and perhaps even resented. As one federal court of appeals has put it: "Cases are not decided by timid panels who are in doubt of the results reached. Attempts to overcome deficiencies in the record or reiteration of previously rejected legal theories will not prompt a change of mind."[62] In extremely busy courts that issue rulings unaccompanied by reasons, there is no way of knowing whether your point was overlooked or misunderstood—and a motion for reconsideration may stand a better (though still not a hardy) chance of success. Whatever the court, never use a motion for reconsideration "as a means to argue new facts or issues that inexcusably were not presented to the court in the matter previously decided."[63]

The brief supporting a motion for reconsideration should in some respects resemble a petition for certiorari: you're seeking discretionary action and must persuade the court to exercise its discretion. Zero in on the one or two respects in which the judgment or ruling mistakes the facts or the law, and state specifically how it needs to be amended. You must do this, needless to say, in the most respectful and

---

62 *Westcot Corp. v. Edo Corp.*, 857 F.2d 1387, 1388 (10th Cir. 1988).
63 *Bhatnagar v. Surrendra Overseas Ltd.*, 52 F.3d 1220, 1231 (3d Cir. 1995).

nonaccusatory manner. Don't make the common mistake of falling into a carping, querulous tone. You're trying to help the court, on further reflection, get it right—not complaining about the court's getting it wrong.

Sometimes you may have no hope of getting an appellate panel to change its mind, but may be convinced that the panel's judgment would not be supported by the full court. If that is so, seek reconsideration (rehearing) en banc.[64] In such a motion it is particularly important to emphasize how the judgment is in conflict with the judgment of an earlier panel of the same court, how it places the court in disagreement with other intermediate appellate courts, and how the point of law at issue is of general significance.

Sometimes an opinion may misdescribe your client in a manner that can have adverse consequences—for example, mistakenly calling your corporate client a "personal corporation," which might worsen the shareholders' position in an unrelated tax audit. Or the opinion may misstate uncontested facts in a way that places your client in a bad light. Before wheeling out the artillery of a motion for reconsideration to correct such details, see if there is some other accepted manner of bringing them to the court's attention. In the Supreme Court of the United States, for example, the slip opinion released on the day of the judgment invites the world at large to point out errors of detail before the opinion is published in the United States Reports. Of course, copies

---

64 *See, e.g.*, Fed. R. App. P. 35.

of all correspondence suggesting changes must be sent to the other side.

114. Learn from your mistakes.

When argument is over, recall it. Conduct a postmortem with a friend or associate who was present. Jot down the respects in which you know you fell short, and consider how you could improve in those respects next time.

115. Plan on developing a reputation for excellence.

Don't take the court's judgment as the measure of your competence. When the judgment is announced, and it turns out you have lost, don't take it too much to heart; and when it turns out you have won, don't let it go to your head. The court, after all, makes its judgment on the basis of what it believes to be the law, not on the basis of which side presented the better argument. The odds are always better with skilled counsel; but it's not uncommon for a client to win *despite* a shoddy lawyer, or to lose *despite* a superb lawyer—because neither the bad argument nor the excellent argument could obscure the clarity of the law or alter the facts.

> "[P]erhaps the most valuable thing the lawyer brings into the courtroom when he is an advocate is his reputation. His reputation for candor and soundness is worth three points in his brief and a marvelous opening for his oral argument. If his reputation is bad, I don't care what he says or how he says it—he is climbing a glass mountain in shoes covered with oil."
> —Hon. Charles D. Breitel

Whatever the outcome of the case, the quality of your performance will have advanced or hindered your career. If you appear before the court in question with any frequency, the judges will remember you as fair-minded, reliable, and trustworthy—or the opposite. If the former, they will be more likely to grant discretionary review in a case that you assert to be worth considering; and when you appear to argue, the credibility you have developed will give you a leg-up. If your argument has been uninformative and misleading, you may well begin your next case at a disadvantage.

So look upon this profession of advocacy as a long-term continuum, each individual case not standing in isolation but profiting from and building upon your prior success. Argue not just for the day but for reputation.

Sources for Inset Quotations

Frontispiece: T.W. Wakeling, *The Oral Component of Appellate Work*, 5 Dalhousie L.J. 584, 586 (1979).

Frontispiece: Dionysius of Halicarnassus, *On Literary Composition* (ca. 30 B.C.), in *Dionysius of Halicarnassus: The Critical Essays* (Stephen Usher trans., 1985).

Page 5: Samuel E. Gates, "Hot Bench or Cold Bench: When the Court Has Not Read the Brief Before Oral Argument," in *Counsel on Appeal* 107, 112–13 (Arthur A. Charpentier ed., 1968).

Page 8: E. Barrett Prettyman Jr., *Supreme Court Advocacy: Random Thoughts in a Day of Time Restrictions*, Litig., Winter 1978, at 16, 18–19.

Page 13: Hon. Wiley B. Rutledge, *The Appellate Brief*, 28 ABA J. 251, 254 (1942).

Page 16: Cicero, "De Inventione" (ca. 87 B.C.), in *De Inventione; De Optimo Genere Oratorum; Topica* 125 (H.M. Hubbell trans., 1949; repr. 2006).

Page 19: Hon. Patricia M. Wald, *19 Tips from 19 Years on the Appellate Bench*, 1 J. App. Prac. & Proc. 7, 21 (1999).

Page 21: Frederick Bernays Wiener, *Essentials of an Effective Appellate Brief*, 17 Geo. W. L. Rev. 143, 147 (1949).

Page 23: Quintilian, 2 *Institutio Oratoria* 303 (ca. A.D. 95; H.E. Butler trans., 1922).

Page 24: Demetrius of Phalerum, "On Style," (ca. 300 B.C.; C.M.A. Grube trans.), in *Readings in Classical Rhetoric* 256, 258 (Thomas W. Benson & Michael H. Prosser eds., 1988).

Page 26: Hon. Luke M. McAmis, *The Lawyer and the Court of Appeals,* 24 Tenn. L. Rev. 279, 281–82 (1956).

Page 32: Hon. Alex Kozinski, *The Wrong Stuff,* 1992 BYU L. Rev. 325, 333.

Page 34: T.W. Wakeling, *The Oral Component of Appellate Work,* 5 Dalhousie L.J. 584, 590 (1979).

Page 43: F.C.S. Schiller (as quoted in Jerome Frank, *Courts on Trial* 184–85 (1949)).

Page 61: Rt. Hon. Lord Birkett, "The Art of Advocacy: Character and Skills for the Trial of Cases" (1948), in *Advocacy and the King's English* 919, 932 (George Rossman ed., 1960).

Page 69: Arthur Schopenhauer, *Essays and Aphorisms* 199 (1851; R.J. Hollingdale trans., 1970).

Page 70: Quintilian, *Quintilian on the Teaching of Speaking and Writing: Translations from Books One, Two, and Ten of the Institution Oratoria* 155 (ca. A.D. 95; James J. Murphy trans., 1987).

Page 73: Robert L. Stern, *Appellate Practice in the United States* 332 (1981).

Page 77: Hon. Fred M. Vinson, *Work of the U.S. Supreme Court,* Tex. B.J., Dec. 1949, at 551, 552.

Page 81: Quintilian, *Quintilian on the Teaching of Speaking and Writing: Translations from Books One, Two, and Ten of the Institution Oratoria* 147 (ca. A.D. 95; James J. Murphy trans., 1987).

Page 83: Frank E. Cooper, *Stating the Issue in Appellate Briefs: A Matter of Legal Strategy,* 39 ABA J. 13, 13 (1953).

Page 94: Harold R. Medina, "The Oral Argument on Appeal" (1934), in *Advocacy and the King's English* 537, 540 (George Rossman ed., 1960).

Page 97: Robert L. Stern, *Appellate Practice in the United States* 277 (1981).

Page 99: Hon. Alex Kozinski, *The Wrong Stuff,* 1992 BYU L. Rev. 325, 327.

Page 107: Hon. Irving R. Kaufman, *Appellate Advocacy in the Federal Courts,* 79 F.R.D. 165, 169 (1978).

Page 110: Sherman Kent, *Writing History* 61 (1941).

Page 112: Cicero, "De Inventione" (ca. 87 B.C.), in *De Inventione; De Optimo Genere Oratorum; Topica* 121 (H.M. Hubbell trans., 1949; repr. 2006).

Page 114: Hon. Wiley B. Rutledge, *The Appellate Brief,* 28 ABA J. 251, 255 (1942).

Page 120: John Algeo, "More Acronyms," 51 *Am. Speech* 152 (1976).

Page 126: Howard C. Westwood, "Brief Writing" (1935), in *Advocacy and the King's English* 563, 565 (George Rossman ed., 1960).

Page 128: Hon. Daniel M. Friedman, "Winning on Appeal," in *Appellate Practice Manual* 129, 133 (Priscilla Anne Schwab ed., 1992).

Page 136: Mark P. Painter, *The Legal Writer* 35 (2002).

Page 142: Henry S. Wilcox, *Foibles of the Bar* 135 (1906).

Page 145: Frank H. Vizetelly, *How to Use English* 20 (1933).

Page 147: Hon. William H. Rehnquist, *From Webster to Word-Processing: The Ascendance of the Appellate Brief,* 1 J. App. Prac. & Proc. 1, 5 (1999).

Page 151: F. Trowbridge Vom Baur, *The Art of Brief Writing,* Scrivener, 1975–1976, at 1, 3.

Page 154: Hon. Murray I. Gurfein, "Appellate Advocacy, Modern Style," in *Appellate Practice Manual* 256, 256 (Priscilla Anne Schwab ed., 1992).

Page 155: John W. Davis, *The Argument of an Appeal*, 26 ABA J. 895, 897 (1940).

Page 157: Rt. Hon. Lord Macmillan, "Some Observations on the Art of Advocacy" (1933), in *Law and Other Things* 200, 206–07 (1937).

Page 159: Greville Janner, *Janner's Complete Speechmaker* 128 (1981).

Page 160: Ronald J. Rychlak, *Effective Appellate Advocacy: Tips from the Teams*, 66 Miss. L.J. 527, 530 n.3 (1997).

Page 162: Hon. Robert H. Jackson, *Advocacy Before the Supreme Court: Suggestions for Effective Case Presentations*, 37 ABA J. 801, 862 (1951).

Page 164: H. Graham Morison, *Oral Argument of Appeal*, 10 Wash. & Lee L. Rev. 1, 7 (1953).

Page 166: Edward L. Lascher, *Oral Argument for Fun and Profit*, Cal. St. B.J., July–Aug. 1973, at 398, 402.

Page 168: Hon. Richard A. Posner, *Convincing a Federal Court of Appeals*, Litig., Winter 1999, at 3, 62.

Page 170: Carter G. Phillips, *Advocacy Before the United States Supreme Court*, 15 T.M. Cooley L. Rev. 177, 191 (1988).

Page 172: Erwin N. Griswold, *Appellate Advocacy with Particular Reference to the United States Supreme Court*, N.Y. St. B.J., Oct. 1972, at 375, 377.

Page 174: Frederick Bernays Wiener, *Oral Advocacy*, 62 Harv. L. Rev. 56, 59–60 (1948).

Page 175: E. Barrett Prettyman Jr., *Supreme Court Advocacy: Random Thoughts in a Day of Time Restrictions*, Litig., Winter 1978, at 16, 19.

Page 178: Hon. Myron H. Bright, *The Changing Nature of the Federal Appeals*, 65 F.R.D. 496, 507 (1975).

Page 180: Piero Calamandrei, *Eulogy of Judges* 35 (J.C. Adams & C.A. Phillips Jr. trans., 1942; repr. 1992).

Page 184: Rex E. Lee, *Oral Argument in the Supreme Court*, 72 ABA J., June 1986, at 60, 61.

Page 186: Watson Clay, "Presenting Your Case to the Court of Appeals" (1952), in *Advocacy and the King's English* 330, 332 (George Rossman ed., 1960).

Page 189: Hon. Simon H. Rifkind, "Appellate Courts Compared," in *Counsel on Appeal* 163, 187 (Arthur A. Charpentier ed., 1968).

Page 191: Hon. William H. Rehnquist, *Oral Advocacy*, 27 S. Tex. L. Rev. 289, 302 (1986).

Page 193: William J. Boyce, *Reflections on Going to the Show*, 17 App. Advocate (report of the State Bar of Texas Appellate Section), Summer 2004, at 21, 22–23.

Page 194: Hon. Thurgood Marshall, "The Federal Appeal," in *Counsel on Appeal* 139, 150 (Arthur A. Charpentier ed., 1968).

Page 195: Hon. Irving R. Kaufman, *Appellate Advocacy in the Federal Courts*, 79 F.R.D. 165, 171–72 (1978).

Page 196: Rex E. Lee, *Oral Argument in the Supreme Court*, 72 ABA J., June 1986, at 60, 60.

Page 197: Keith Evans, *The Language of Advocacy* 75–76 (1998).

Page 199: Talbot D'Alemberte, *Oral Argument: The Continuing Conversation*, Litig., Winter 1999, at 12, 67.

Page 205: Hon. Charles D. Breitel, "A Summing Up," in *Counsel on Appeal* 193, 205–06 (Arthur A. Charpentier ed., 1968).

Recommended Sources

General English-Language Dictionaries
(latest edition unless otherwise noted)

- *The American Heritage Dictionary of the English Language* (thorough, with good usage notes).
- *Merriam-Webster's Collegiate Dictionary* (used by most book publishers, but be wary of its permissive usage notes).
- *The Random House Dictionary of the English Language.*
- *The Shorter Oxford English Dictionary.*
- *Webster's New World College Dictionary* (used by most newspapers).
- *Webster's Second New International Dictionary* (William Allan Neilson ed., 1934) (still quite sound on historical matters, and exhaustive on traditional legal and literary terms).
- *Webster's Third New International Dictionary* (Philip B. Gove ed., 1961) (scholarly but infamously permissive in neglecting to include accurate usage tags—so use it discriminatingly).

Usage Guides

- Theodore M. Bernstein, *The Careful Writer: A Modern Guide to English Usage* (1965).
- Mark Davidson, *Right, Wrong, and Risky: A Dictionary of Today's American English Usage* (2006).
- H.W. Fowler, *A Dictionary of Modern English Usage* (Ernest Gowers ed., 2d ed. 1965).
- Bryan A. Garner, *A Dictionary of Modern Legal Usage* (2d ed. 1995).
- Bryan A. Garner, *Garner's Modern American Usage* (2d ed. 2003).

- Barbara Wallraff, *Word Court: Wherein Verbal Virtue Is Rewarded, Crimes Against the Language Are Punished, and Poetic Justice Is Done* (2001).

Thesauruses

- *The Oxford American Writer's Thesaurus* (Christine A. Lindberg ed., 2004).
- J.I. Rodale, *The Synonym Finder* (Laurence Urdang ed., rev. ed. 1986).
- *Roget's International Thesaurus* (Robert L. Chapman ed., 1992).
- *Roget's Thesaurus of English Words and Phrases* (George Davidson ed., 2006).

Grammar

- George O. Curme, *A Grammar of the English Language*, 2 vols. (1935; much reprinted).
- Bryan A. Garner, "Grammar and Usage," ch. 5 of *The Chicago Manual of Style* (15th ed. 2003) (a 92-page restatement of English grammar).
- Edward D. Johnson, *The Handbook of Good English* (1982).
- Patricia T. O'Conner, *Woe Is I: The Grammarphobe's Guide to Better English in Plain English* (2d ed. 2004).
- John B. Opdycke, *Harper's English Grammar* (Stewart Benedict ed., 1965).
- John E. Warriner, *English Composition and Grammar: Complete Course* (1988).

General Writing Guidance
- Rudolf Flesch, *The Art of Readable Writing* (1949).
- Robert Graves & Alan Hodge, *The Reader over Your Shoulder* (2d ed. 1947).
- William Strunk & E.B. White, *The Elements of Style* (4th ed. 2000).
- John R. Trimble, *Writing with Style: Conversations on the Art of Writing* (2d ed. 2000).
- William Zinsser, *On Writing Well* (6th ed. 2006).

Legal Writing Style
- Bryan A. Garner, *The Elements of Legal Style* (2d ed. 2002).
- Bryan A. Garner, *The Redbook: A Manual on Legal Style* (2d ed. 2006).
- Richard C. Wydick, *Plain English for Lawyers* (5th ed. 2005).

Editing Guidance
- *The Chicago Manual of Style* (15th ed. 2003) (the classic American text).
- William A. Sabin, *The Gregg Reference Manual* (10th ed. 2004).
- *Words into Type* (3d ed. 1974).

Classical Rhetoric
- Aristotle, *The Art of Rhetoric* (ca. 330 B.C.; H.C. Lawson-Tancred trans., rev. ed. 2004); or Aristotle, *Rhetoric* (Lane Cooper trans., 1932).
- Marcus Tullius Cicero, *On Oratory and Orators* (ca. 55 B.C.; J.S. Watson trans., 1986).
- Demetrius of Phalerum, *On Style* (ca. 300 B.C.; T.A. Moxon trans., 1943).

- Quintilian, *Quintilian on the Teaching of Speaking and Writing: Translations from Books One, Two, and Ten of the Institution Oratoria* (ca. A.D. 95; James J. Murphy trans., 1987).
- *Readings in Classical Rhetoric* (Thomas W. Benson & Michael H. Prosser eds., 1988).

Modern Guides to Classical Rhetoric
- William J. Brandt, *The Rhetoric of Argumentation* (1970).
- Edward P.J. Corbett, *Classical Rhetoric for the Modern Student* (4th ed. 1998).
- Winifred Bryan Horner, *Rhetoric in the Classical Tradition* (1988).
- James J. Murphy, *A Synoptic History of Classical Rhetoric* (1983).
- Halford Ryan, *Classical Communication for the Contemporary Communicator* (1992).
- Brian Vickers, *In Defense of Rhetoric* (1988).
- Richard M. Weaver, *The Ethics of Rhetoric* (1985).

Brief-Writing
- Bryan A. Garner, *The Winning Brief* (2d ed. 2004).
- Girvan Peck, *Writing Persuasive Briefs* (1984).
- Frederick B. Wiener, *Briefing and Arguing Federal Appeals* (rev. ed. 1967).

Public Speaking
- Reid Buckley, *Speaking in Public* (1988).
- Ron Hoff, *"I Can See You Naked"* (1992).
- Louis Nizer, *Thinking on Your Feet* (1940).
- Peggy Noonan, *Simply Speaking* (1998).
- Charles Osgood, *Osgood on Speaking* (1988).
- Jack Valenti, *Speak Up with Confidence* (2002).

Recommended Sources

Oral Argument
- John W. Davis, *The Argument of an Appeal*, 26 ABA J. 895 (1940).
- David C. Frederick, *Supreme Court and Appellate Advocacy* 101 (2003).
- Bryan A. Garner, *The Winning Oral Argument* (2007).
- John M. Harlan, *What Part Does the Oral Argument Play in the Conduct of an Appeal?*, 41 Cornell L.Q. 6 (1955).
- Robert H. Jackson, *Advocacy Before the Supreme Court*, 37 ABA J. 801, 863 (1951).
- Rex E. Lee, *Oral Argument in the Supreme Court*, ABA J., June 1986, at 60, 62.
- Harold R. Medina, *The Oral Argument on Appeal*, 20 ABA J. 139 (1934).
- E. Barrett Prettyman, *Some Observations Concerning Appellate Advocacy*, 39 Va. L. Rev. 285, 302 (1953).
- E. Barrett Prettyman Jr., *Supreme Court Advocacy: Random Thoughts in a Day of Time Restrictions*, Litig., Winter 1978, at 16.
- William H. Rehnquist, *Oral Advocacy*, 27 S. Tex. L. Rev. 289 (1986).

Logic and Critical Thinking
- Monroe C. Beardsley, *Thinking Straight* (4th ed. 1975).
- Neil Browne & Stuart Keeley, *Asking the Right Questions: A Guide to Critical Thinking* (8th ed. 2006).
- Edward de Bono, *De Bono's Thinking Course* (rev. ed. 1994).
- Alec Fisher, *The Logic of Real Arguments* (2d ed. 2004).
- Antony Flew, *How to Think Straight* (2d ed. 1998).

Legal Reasoning

- Wilson Huhn, *The Five Types of Legal Argument* (2002).
- O.C. Jensen, *The Nature of Legal Argument* (1957).
- Edward H. Levi, *An Introduction to Legal Reasoning* (1949).
- Douglas Lind, *Logic and Legal Reasoning* (2001).
- Clarence Morris, *How Lawyers Think* (1937).
- Kenneth J. Vandevelde, *Thinking Like a Lawyer: An Introduction to Legal Reasoning* (1996).

Standards of Decision

- Harry T. Edwards & Linda A. Elliott, *Federal Standards of Review: Review of District Court Decisions and Agency Actions* (2007).

Index

Index

Index

Index

Index

Index

Index

Index

Index

Index